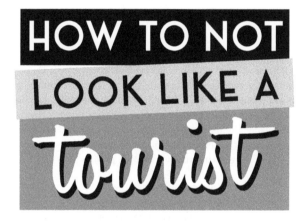

HOW TO NOT LOOK LIKE A *tourist*

UNLOCKING YOUR HIDDEN POWER FOR OVERTOURISM SOLUTIONS

ALYSE • THE INVISIBLE TOURIST

How to Not Look Like a Tourist:
Unlocking Your Hidden Power for Overtourism Solutions

Published by The Invisible Tourist
www.theinvisibletourist.com
Copyright © Alyse • The Invisible Tourist 2021
Book Cover Design Copyright © Alyse • The Invisible Tourist 2021

ISBN 9780645229288 (Paperback)
ISBN 9780645229233 (Hardcover)
ISBN 9780645229219 (eBook)

 A catalogue record for this book is available from the National Library of Australia

Neither the author nor publisher shall be liable or responsible for any loss or damage allegedly arising from any information or suggestion in this book. So far as the author is aware, the information given is correct and up to date at the time of publication. Neither the publisher nor author assumes responsibility for errors or changes that occur after publication.

*

*Dedicated to those who have
ever rolled their eyes at tourists
and know we all deserve better.*

- Alyse

CONTENTS

CONTENTS

INTRODUCTION

She was much smaller than I had envisioned, but lovely nonetheless. Perched upon balancing boulders in Copenhagen's Langelinie Bay, I approached Hans Christian Andersen's *Little Mermaid* basking in the midday sun. Having all but a moment of tranquility to appreciate this bronze statue, a coach pulled up on the road beside me carrying a large group of foreign tourists.

Suddenly I was surrounded, fighting for a patch of prized real estate to capture a shot of this Danish icon. But a simple photo wasn't enough for these people. Wearing flashy shoes and sporting designer handbags on their forearms, they clambered across water (and each other) on the uneven rocky surface to actually *be* in the shot.

Posing this way and that, climbing on top of the statue whilst their counterpart back on dry land took their sweet time capturing several shots, they did whatever it took in this unwritten contest to outdo each other - everyone else be damned. I left in disgust and before long I realised this mass tourist behaviour was not unique to Copenhagen...

Endless snaking queues of tourists hoped to catch a glimpse of Paris from atop the Eiffel Tower. Thousands of tourists simultaneously disembarked from cruise ships on the ancient European port towns of Dubrovnik, Venice and Santorini. Irresponsible tourists carved their names into the Arashiyama Bamboo Groves in Kyoto, a UNESCO World Heritage site. Heck, there was even a lengthy queue to reach the top of Mount Everest, one of the most uninhabitable places on our planet.

In 2019 more people were travelling across our globe than ever before, especially in large crowds cloaked in anonymity. A relatively new word had begun to fill the pages of news sites, travel publications and was sitting on the lips of many within the tourism industry: *Overtourism.*

After careful first-hand observations of the ways travel has changed globally throughout the last decade (particularly since the Global Financial Crisis of 2008), I noticed some worrying trends. As someone who had travelled long before social media and the sharing economy, I witnessed an unsustainable shift in attitudes of tourists as globetrotting became more focussed on the individual and profits rather than the destination itself.

Due to an increasing passion to spread awareness of the issues stemming from these trends and what we can do as tourists to avoid them, in 2017 I created and launched The Invisible Tourist into the blogosphere. In keeping with my *invisible* theme, I decided to refrain from posting photos of myself in order to let my experiences speak for themselves. Around one year later it grew into more than I could have ever imagined and as a result I've been professionally blogging ever since!

Having visited over 250 cities across four continents, through my blog I've helped over 2.5 million tourists discover the benefits of *invisible tourism* by sharing my detailed personal itineraries, honest advice and unpopular truths from my experiences across our globe. I've never been robbed or had anything stolen, and have often been mistaken as a local by fellow tourists. I'd like to think it's because I use my proven strategy to *blend in* wherever I go.

In early 2020, international travel ground to a complete halt for the first time in living memory. Trying to be an optimist in an unthinkable situation (which, believe me, has been more difficult than I'd like to admit), I prefer to think we may have been given a unique chance to turn lemons into lemonade by examining and reflecting on the mistakes of the past.

The timing has never been better to collectively take action and implement changes to improve the future tourism industry for visitors, locals, fauna, and our environment. With one in ten jobs globally counting on the existence of the tourism industry combined with the benefits it can bring, a world without tourism altogether is not the answer.

After a year of research, examining statistics and reflecting upon my own first-hand knowledge from on the ground, I created this handbook for curious tourists who wish to travel more responsibly – and share the growing concerns about negative impacts tourism has had on local communities. After all, our vacation destination is someone's home, not just a pretty picture on social media. How can we tackle these issues moving forward?

Unbeknownst to most tourists, there is a hidden power within them. They just need to know how to go against the grain to find it! This book will explain how we arrived at overtourism and the issues it has caused before revealing how you can unlock this hidden power to use as a force for good.

In the first half of this book I'm going to discuss the unsustainable aspects of travel and why they became problematic – you may be surprised at the speed in which they came to be! In the second half of the book I'll be sharing my insights from over a decade travelling the world to help combat these trends, amplify the positive aspects of tourism and provide you with the framework for planning more meaningful travel experiences. It's a win-win for yourself and locals, too.

By way of setting expectations, this book focuses on the social, economical and cultural impacts of overtourism and lessons learnt from my personal experiences. Many other authors have written extensively on the subject of the wider environmental impacts also associated with tourism, to which you can find helpful resources in the Further Reading section at this book's conclusion.

I hope you find this handbook an informative, useful companion to help you better *blend in* next time you book your tickets, pack a suitcase and set off on an exciting adventure!

PART I

THE CHALLENGES WITH TOURISM

"We travel not to escape life, but for life not to escape us."
- Anonymous.

What's my most favourite thing? I absolutely *love* being a tourist, just not in the way you may think. Nothing compares to that rush of touching down in an unexplored city; the medley of emotions felt when laying eyes on a painting I've yearned to visit for years; the excitement of savouring new cuisines; the anticipation of first-hand knowledge I'll gain from meeting people of different cultures.

There are plenty of things to love about being a tourist, which is why I don't mind calling myself one. Being a tourist is a privilege not afforded to all, thus I'm mindful to never take it for granted. However, I've never loved *looking* like a tourist so I always strive to blend in as best as possible wherever I go. My guess is you hope to achieve this, too!

Why is it Bad to Look Like a Tourist?

If you've followed me for a while you'll be familiar with me saying, *no one likes an annoying tourist.* Generally speaking they're loud, sometimes pushy, and swarm out of huge tour buses into crowded cities all at once causing disruptions to the local way of life.

It can be embarrassing to be unintentionally grouped into the "annoying" category by locals, as problems can arise from looking and acting like a stereotypical tourist:

- **Can seem disrespectful:** Being overly loud, oblivious to their surroundings or drawing unwanted attention by acting like a tourist means they've not bothered to learn local customs or etiquette, which can be a display of disrespect.
- **Treated differently:** Dressing like a tourist can make it evident they aren't a local and can lead to unfavourable treatment in some stores or restaurants. Being charged more for a meal or not given the same kind of attention or respect as a local can occur because tourists are a dime a dozen, unlikely to return.
- **A target for scams:** It can be obvious they're on holiday and therefore have a flashing ATM sign above their foreheads in the eyes of those with malicious intent. Looking like a distracted sucker to those who deceive tourists for a living can make them a target for pickpockets and other types of tourist scams. Unfortunately, it happens!
- **Unaware of negative tourism impacts:** Not realising the unseen damage of travelling in popular ways that are culturally and environmentally unsustainable.
- **Unaware of what they're actually missing out on:** Only visiting the famous tourist attractions during busy periods can lead to a shallow, inauthentic experience of a destination. They don't know what they don't know!

Okay, not everyone intends to be *that* type of tourist I've described above who clearly stands out, however many don't realise there is room for improvement with the choices they make. Why is it an issue if the average tourist prefers to:

- Stay in unregulated homestay accommodation in popular cities?

- Allow themselves to be whisked around multiple destinations on large tourist coaches of 50 people?
- Embark on cheap day trips to cities known to suffer from overtourism?
- Take package holidays on huge cruise ships that only spend a few hours at busy port cities?
- Enjoy interacting with animals used in tourism?

During my earliest travel days back in 2008, I made some of the above errors in judgement. Having since learnt from them, I'll be detailing why these choices became issues globally in the first half of this book. I discovered things that may seem harmless at first can actually have detrimental impacts on locals' way of life and our environment.

In saying that, how can we visit a destination without standing out as a tourist? By taking steps to be *invisible*, of course.

What is an Invisible Tourist?

An Invisible Tourist is someone who makes a conscious effort to "blend in" when travelling. I started using this term to raise awareness to the importance of minimising negative impacts tourism has on locals, their communities, their culture and environment.

Invisible Tourists actively seek to resolve challenges resulting from tourism by asking these questions:
- How can we continue to travel yet minimise the disruption to locals?
- How can we help preserve the identities and culture of the places we visit?
- What can we do to give back to locals whilst we're travelling?

If you want to enjoy all the perks of being a tourist without looking like one to help curb overtourism issues, within the pages of this handbook you will learn how to:

- Examine why and how tourism has changed throughout the decades
- Plan the perfect stress-free trip every time, including ways to reduce disappointment
- Enjoy popular destinations without contributing to overcrowding
- Feel fulfilled by personal, authentic encounters with locals whilst helping their businesses
- Radiate confidence to avoid pickpockets and scammers for a safe travel experience
- Preserve local cultures and identities instead of diluting them
- Protect attractions of significant cultural heritage and the environment.

Are you ready to discover why *blending in* when abroad can overcome tourism challenges in our modern age? Drumroll, please... Let's get started!

PART II

HOW WE ARRIVED AT OVERTOURISM: A BACKGROUND

"Those who do not learn from history are doomed to repeat it."
- George Santayana.

It's a story almost as old as time itself. Our ancestors have always travelled and been curious about this wonderful world we live in. For now, I'm not talking about early explorers or merchants that used the Old Silk Road to trade goods. Nor do I mean religious pilgrimages which involved extensive journeys to spiritual places.

I'm referring to travelling for enjoyment and education. For instance, great cities such as St Petersburg, Russia were inspired by leaders who were fascinated by the Baroque architecture of Versailles and the culture of France.

The word *overtourism* was initially coined in 2016 by travel media company Skift, although it wasn't widely used until two years later to describe the far-reaching negative impacts of more people visiting a destination than it could handle.

To put things into context, let's take a quick journey back through time to significant milestones that shaped the tourism industry until early 2020. To understand how we can move forward, we need to peer backward to comprehend how the tourism boom came to be.

This small timeline is an overview on the evolution of aviation and technological changes in travel during the 20th and 21st centuries. As an example, it's amazing to think it once took my grandfather several months on a boat to reach Australia from Italy after WWII. Today, that same lengthy journey can be done in around 24 hours on a commercial flight.

We've come an unimaginably long way in a relatively short time! As tourists, this can mean shifting our mindsets towards making beneficial choices could have an influence sooner than we realise.

Travel Milestones from the 20th & 21st Centuries

- **1900** - American Wright Brothers develop and test the first working aircraft, paving the way for the future of aviation
- **1911** - Italy is the first to use planes for military purposes in the Italian-Turkish war in Libya
- **1922** - First flight across the South Atlantic is made from Lisbon to Rio de Janeiro
- **1928** - Australian Sir Charles Kingford Smith makes the first flight across the Pacific Ocean in 3 stages
- **1939** - Development of the jet engine by Germany and Britain
- **1945** - Commercial aviation increased rapidly with ex-military aircraft
- **1956** - Jet Age is born. USSR's Aeroflot was the first sustained regular jet service. Boeing 707 enters service
- **1961** - Russian Yuri Gagarin becomes the first man into outer space to orbit the planet
- **1969** - American Neil Armstrong is the first man to step foot on the moon. The first Boeing 747 jets off with Pan Am
- **1972** - Founding of Carnival Cruise Line (the TV show *Love Boat* helped cruising become mainstream)
- **1989** - Fall of the Berlin Wall opened up Eastern Europe

- **1992** - The recent fall of the Berlin Wall lead to the development of the Rhine-Main-Danube Canal and river cruising
- **1994** - Carlson Wagonlit Travel forms from a merger of two large agencies, resulting in mega travel agencies
- **1996** - Launch of Disney Cruise Line, making travel more accessible and mainstream to families
- **1996** - Expedia and Booking.com online travel agencies are launched
- **2000** - TripAdvisor launches forum for travellers to post their own opinions and experiences to help inform others
- **2001** - 9/11 rocks the world, changing security in aviation for travellers. China joined the World Trade Organisation
- **2006** - Facebook begins exponential growth at 12 million users worldwide
- **2007** - Apple launches the iPhone, which is about to revolutionise everything including how people travel
- **2008** - US stock market crashes, causing the Global Financial Crisis (GFC) and overall drop in travel demand
- **2010** - Instagram is launched, aesthetic photography begins influencing travel decisions
- **2015** - Travel activity platform Klook launches in Asia to connect travellers with local experiences
- **2018** - Royal Caribbean launches Symphony of the Seas, the world's largest cruise ship with over 5,000 capacity
- **2019** - FlightRadar24 records the highest number of global flights in one day, at over 225,000 on 24th July
- **2020** - Australia's national carrier QANTAS turns 100 as global travel grinds to a standstill during a pandemic.

Trends in Travel

So, what trends have occurred around travel to make significant changes in the industry?

We're now going to focus on the ways travel has changed since the 2008 Global Financial Crisis (GFC) specifically. For most people before the GFC, travel was considered more of an occasional luxury and used to be a big deal. Some folks would see loved ones off at airport Departures and they'd return some weeks later with stories of adventure and exotic souvenirs from what they considered the trip of a lifetime.

In recent years, that trip of a lifetime could happen annually, and sometimes more often. According to statistics from the World Bank[1], in 2009 there were 911 million international tourists. Just 9 years later in 2018, this number skyrocketed to 1.4 billion.

Perhaps if you weren't travelling before 2010, you may not be aware of the differences to tourism some trends have caused. How did we go from travel being reserved for the upper classes of society to overtourism?

A number of contributing factors led to travel becoming accessible to groups of people it hadn't been just a generation before. Let's take a look at each.

Travel Becoming More Accessible & Affordable

I was surprised to learn that in 1945, it took 130 weeks for the average Australian to earn enough for the lowest airfare from Sydney to London. In 2009, this time decreased to just 1.7 weeks.

In addition to social media and mass tourism becoming normalised, the combination of the rise of budget airlines, the popularity of the sharing economy, the growth of the middle class in Asia, huge cruise ships, the explosion of homestay accommodation services and a growth in accessibility options created the perfect storm for an unsustainable tourism boom. I've broken them down below.

i) Rise of the Middle Class in Asia

In 2011, the total number of middle class in Asia overtook that of Europe. The global middle class can be defined as households with an income of USD $10 - $110 per day, according to Brookings Institution.

A study[2] by the World Economic Forum concluded that in 2020 the middle class in Asia grew to 2 billion people, taking their global share to 54%. This number is forecast[3] to increase to 3.5 billion by 2030. In contrast, the middle class in the Americas is stagnating, if not decreasing, having only 17% share of the global middle class in 2020.

According to the BBC[4], tourists from Asia became the biggest source of global tourism spending in 2013, with shopping and purchasing souvenirs to bring home to relatives high on their wishlists.

ii) Rise of the Budget Airline

Don't need to check a bag? Happy to skip a meal on your flight? No worries, low-cost carriers have your back. The rise of the budget airline from the early 2000's meant travelling became accessible to more people, with the promise of taking them to destinations they would not have dreamt of just ten years earlier.

Founded in 1984, it could be argued that the UK's Ryanair spearheaded the budget airline movement[5]. It wasn't until ten years later their first competitor, EasyJet, came along. This fierce competition combined with the addition of other budget airlines such as WizzAir (2003), Vueling (2004) and WowAir (2011) resulted in outbound flights to Europe becoming cheaper than a one way ticket within the UK. I know what I'd choose!

In 2015 the BBC revealed[6] budget airlines were incentivised by local airport officials to encourage more passenger arrivals. In addition to take-off and landing fees, airlines were charged €5.35 per passenger up to 100,000 for a calendar year. If an airline was able to exceed three million passengers, this fee fell by half to €2.24.

iii) Cruise Ships Grew Bigger (& Better?)

I couldn't be happier the day I'd booked a cruise around the Greek Islands! My partner and I wanted to enjoy the convenience of a floating hotel while cruising the Aegean Sea, experiencing the ancient beauty of islands such as Crete, Mykonos and Rhodes. Yet I was especially thrilled for the chance to revisit Santorini, an island I hold dear and was fortunate to have spent a week exploring a few years prior.

After digging around for the cruise's exact sailing schedule, my excitement quickly turned to disappointment when I learnt we'd only be spending an afternoon - 3 hours to be precise - in Santorini. This meant I'd miss out on visiting the Akrotiri Museum I'd longed to see since I was last on the island. I soon realised this tight schedule seemed to be the case with most cruises docking outside Fira's Old Town port.

Although our cruise ship was one of the smaller ones (1,600 passengers and around 30,000 tonnes), we still needed to reach the shore via tender boats. If you're not familiar, a tender boat doesn't sing love songs but is a small jet boat to transport passengers from ship to port when the ship is too large to dock at the port itself.

Not realising that tickets to tender boats were allocated on a first-come-first-served-basis, this lengthy process heavily cut into our allocated time on the island. All we had time for was a brief early dinner at our favourite restaurant, ordering the most delicious saganaki cheese we'd had previously (if you hope to visit someday, this was at Zafora restaurant and it has the most enviable views over the caldera).

This whirlwind visit to Santorini made me wonder how brief some of the port stays really are for huge cruise ships carrying 6,000 passengers. How much time would it take for everyone to disembark, and how little of the destination do visitors actually see?

As demand for travelling on cruise ships increased steadily from the 1980's to 1990's, the industry sought to increase capacity. Each new cruise ship grew larger than its predecessor, with industry leaders competing in an endless loop to boast creating the largest cruise vessel in the world.

Holding a fancy title wasn't the only motivation, however. It turns out larger ships were more efficient to operate as well as more profitable. As Stewart Chiron noted in an interview by The Points Guy[7], "The cost to feed passengers went down, the cost to house the passengers went down." As costs went down, customers also demanded more choice for on-board experiences.

To put things into perspective, as I mentioned my little Greek Island cruise ship was 30,000 tonnes. At the turn of the new century the world's biggest cruise ships shot up from weighing 77,000 tonnes to 137,000 tonnes in just a few years.

The world's largest cruise ship was launched in 2018, its characteristics are quite staggering. This floating city weighs in at 228,000 tonnes, carries 9,000 passengers and crew, is 362 metres in length and 18 decks high - that's twice as high as the Washington Monument. But, is bigger necessarily better?

Mega-ships began to dwarf the cities that lay as a backdrop

behind them. In Venice, Italy, waves generated by the ships were causing erosion to already fragile building foundations and relentless disturbance of sediment on the lagoon's seabed. A mechanical issue even caused an out-of-control cruise ship to crash into the docks[8] and a tourist boat in 2019, injuring five passengers.

These modern marvels of engineering towering over the Renaissance structures of Venice prompted local authorities to float the idea (pun intended) of banning oversized cruise ships from entering the lagoon. It was decided that these ships would have to dock on the Italian mainland instead. The events of early 2020 provided the city of Venice a reprieve from these issues before the measures were implemented.

iv) Essentiality of the Internet

The Internet revolutionised travel by eliminating barriers in ways that may never have been thought possible. With the popularity of sites like Expedia and Booking.com growing year-on-year from the late 1990's, would-be travellers could now forgo using a travel agent to research and book holidays on their behalf.

With access to greater choices available and the ability to check anything in seconds, the Internet became a staple for travel planning - before and even during a trip. Once smartphones began to hit the scene from 2008 onwards, research, booking accommodation and flights could all be done seamlessly online in a few steps - conveniently from anywhere - in the palm of our hands.

v) The Explosion of Unregulated Homestay Accommodation Platforms

Unregulated homestay accommodation platforms offered would-be visitors an alternate perspective of a destination than their mainstream counterparts. In their earliest days, the allure of staying in a local's home for a cheaper price to a hotel in popular cities such as Paris, New York and Barcelona was too good for many to resist.

As these services were allowed to flourish unregulated, issues can sprout when the alternative forms part of the mainstream.

In the cases where a host was not present throughout the stay, the majority of tourists using unregulated homestay accommodation (which from now I'll refer to as UHA) failed to realise they were inadvertently taking apartments from local residents. Movements[9] resisting UHA began to sweep through popular destinations and some authorities implemented measures to lessen the negative impacts.

The rapid growth in UHA services resulted in countless illegal listings[10] and companies purchasing entire residential blocks[11] for the sole purpose of renting them short-term to tourists for a premium. Locals were displaced[12] from their own cities by skyrocketing rents and a shortage of long-term rentals on the market.

While I delve into this subject in greater detail later, the popularity of homestay accommodation services grew exponentially[13] after the GFC, increasing options and affordability for tourists.

vi) Growth in Accessibility Options

Universal accessibility at popular tourist attractions has improved over the years, providing opportunities for wheelchair users to experience places that may not have been possible before. As I'm not a specialist in this area, I reached out to someone who is!

The lovely Sylvia Longmire, author of award-winning accessible travel blog, Spin the Globe[14], was kind enough to provide insight into the ways travel has changed for wheelchair users in the past decade in this mini interview.

Alyse: "Have you noticed improvements in terms of wheelchair users' access to travel experiences that may not have been available a decade ago? Are there a wider range of travel opportunities for you today, or fewer?"

Sylvia: "I have definitely noticed improvements in accessibility in various places around the world. For example, now there is an operating elevator at the Parthenon in Athens, and they have created smooth paved areas where wheelchair users can get closer to the ruins.

"More and more ramps are popping up at historical sites that were previously not accessible to wheelchair users, which is a great thing, but we still have a long way to go."

Alyse: "Have there been any kinds of setbacks for wheelchair users in terms of visiting popular attractions such as museums, monuments or participating in cultural experiences? Any challenges you face today that weren't an issue a decade ago?"

Sylvia: "I don't think there has been any regression per se. I mean, opportunities for us to visit more and more places are increasing overall. If anything, there are some issues here and there with non-disabled tourists and locals maybe thinking we are entitled or have some sort of privilege because we get priority access at some locations.

"That, of course, is problematic for us. I would gladly trade my ability to skip the line in some cases for their ability to walk."

Alyse: "Any other important things to note about the ways travel has changed in the past decade for wheelchair users? Have improvements in technology (if any) helped or hindered your travel experiences? Are more wheelchairs users travelling than years prior due to any increased opportunities?"

Sylvia: "Improvements in technology have definitely created many more accessible travel opportunities. For example, there are some phenomenal stair and chair lifts around the world that have this amazing ability to blend right into the architecture.

"And universal design is a real thing. When you make something universally accessible, it's not just especially for wheelchair users. Absolutely anyone and everyone can use it, and I'm sure that senior citizens and mothers with babies in strollers appreciate it as well."

Thank you for sharing your insights, Sylvia!

As Sylvia has confirmed from her first-hand experiences, an increase in universal accessibility over the past decade has created more opportunities in tourism to benefit people with various needs.

Commercialisation of Mass Tourism

It's almost considered a rite of passage for my fellow Australians to take a "Eurotrip" at some point after we finish high school. Ever since I laid eyes on my mum's *Handbook of Art* former school textbook, I had dreamt about far-flung destinations printed on its pages such as Italy, France and the United Kingdom (pssst, keep this book in mind because I'll be referencing it again later).

Once I finished my tertiary studies and was earning a full-time income (which for a graphic design graduate isn't much to write home about), I was determined to save as much as possible to put towards a Eurotrip.
I yearned to admire Michelangelo's intricate masterpiece of the Sistine Chapel's ceiling, cycle past giant windmills and canals of the Dutch countryside, and smirk at the mysterious Mona Lisa in person. A dirt cheap package tour was going to transform my dreams into a reality. Package tours are nothing new. In fact,

some of the first date back to the early 1900's.

Being the first time my partner and I had travelled overseas without our parents, a tour covering 16 countries in two weeks was appealing and affordable. We paid a small deposit and excitedly booked it in. After all, sharing a coach with 50 people meant prices would be very competitive. We weren't the only tourists to have this mindset and each year more young travellers embarked on similar journeys to us.

To meet the rising demand, an increasing number of package tour companies began popping up offering similar experiences. It didn't become obvious until many years later the extent of the impact large tour groups would have on local communities.

From a fresh-faced young tourist's perspective, we discovered these larger tour groups are somewhat impersonal. While we stayed in bigger hotels that could accommodate large groups, we were rushed around to the more touristy spots in a very short timeframe.

While understandable and a little expected, travelling in this way can lead to disappointment and a skewed view of the destination at a glance. In contrast, years later we discovered smaller groups of up to 12 people tend to have extra free time for discovery, explore offbeat areas and enjoy more authentic local experiences.

On a separate note, this "rite of passage" really taught my partner and I what we did (and didn't) like about travelling in large group tours, helping us develop our future travel style. Sure, one coach bussing us all around Europe was convenient, but it also had unforseen downsides.

Knowing what I know now, I wince when I think back to how our large group could have impacted the places we visited (and how everyone on the coach caught the sniffles).

Information Saturation

Before the age of social media, travelling required a lot of time-consuming research, effort and money. Those who wished to travel had no choice but to put in the hard yards to appreciate unique experiences - ample knowledge was required from books, maybe a little online, word of mouth from others. The mystery surrounding travel was a huge drawcard and alluring for the most curious.

Fast forward to today, tourists have become oversaturated with information and it's had the opposite effect of what we may have expected as a result. They don't even need to research where to visit anymore, it's now possible to just turn up somewhere new and create itineraries on the go (not that I would recommend that - but people do it!).

While smartphones have made everything from researching travel inspiration to booking flights and hotels more convenient, this oversaturation of information has also contributed to the decay of the previous mystery and allure of visiting a destination.

Technology & Sharing

Technology has come a long way in shaping how we communicate. Prior to the 2008 GFC, smartphones were just emerging and mobile data was almost non-existent. Sharing apps such as Facebook weren't a thing so people had to wait for their family and friends to return from a trip to hear about it. And, there was no GPS tracking in hire cars, geotagging on Instagram or people making TikTok videos in public spaces for their online followers.

By 2020, it had never been easier to travel around the world and share experiences online. Quite literally, all a tourist needed was money in their bank account and a smartphone equipped with mobile data. They didn't even need to learn any local language as mobile apps could translate on the go, removing the need to interact with locals.

While these modern tools can sometimes be useful before and during a trip, they can also magnify bad trends. Technology and the ability to share things in an instant has led to the problems of social media influencing travel decisions and an obsession with bucket lists and hashtags. Let's take a look at some examples so we can understand what behaviours to avoid in the future.

i) Social media heavily influenced travel decisions

Today's temptation of instant gratification from social media means tourists can chase "likes" and self-validation by sharing anything from what they ate for lunch to selfies in front of monuments. Things are judged primarily on face value in a few seconds, rather than the stories behind the images.

"The Instagram Effect" even meant travellers chose their holiday destinations based on the potential likes[15] they could receive on the platform. "Instagram" tours popped up in Bali, Indonesia[16]; cafés throughout the globe updated their décor to become more "Instagrammable" and some venues feature interactive sections for selfies and Instagram photo opportunities.

Traveller's expectations became so high based on heavily edited social media photos that 2 out of 3 Americans lied about how great their trip was[17]. The obvious lack of prior planning and research resulted in people not knowing how to behave correctly, interact with locals or the significance of what they were visiting.

In the days of travelling with a disposable camera and not knowing how any of the photos would turn out until they were developed at a photography store weeks later, travel was about the experience rather than showcasing it to online followers.

ii) Documenting Bucket Lists & Hashtag Obsessions

With online articles outlining "bucket list" experiences in checklist formats, "Instagrammable" guides to destinations and hashtags like *#doitforthegram*, it drives would-be tourists to photographically document everything and cross off as many as possible in a short timeframe - but without really knowing why. It reminds me of the time I was deliberately elbowed in the ribs in Washington D.C., where a group of tourists were aggressively trying to photograph the Hope Diamond without bothering to read exactly what it was.

The need to be seen has been a driving factor for tourism in younger generations. According to a Forbes UK survey[18], 40% of tourists under 30 said they choose a travel destination based on its popularity on Instagram, with the opportunities for sampling local cuisine and sightseeing coming in at only 9% and 3%, respectively.

In early 2019 an abundant bloom of orange poppies in California led to a small town shutting off its roads to prevent gridlock[19] and damage to the landscape. This was solely caused by people wanting to take photos for their Instagram. Sections of poppies were trampled with budding photographers and their subjects wandering off marked trails. Ironically, these irresponsible actions ruined the very thing these people came to visit and enjoy.

It seems today's tourists are chasing a collection of destinations and the same popular photos as everyone else to achieve a sense of belonging. While this is deeply ingrained within human nature, it begs the question of how authentic these travel experiences really are, especially when only 3% of young tourists choose their destination for sightseeing purposes!

Over the years, the tourism boom has resulted in an increase in "selfie" related deaths and irresponsible tourist behaviour. In 2011, there were only 3 selfie-related deaths recorded. A global study concluded there were 259 selfie-related deaths[20] from 2012 - 2017. Why would people risk their lives or destroy anything in the name of a photo? More examples of the downsides related to hashtag obsessions are:

- **Illegal activity:** Tourists trespassing on farmland in Hokkaido, Japan for photos amongst flower fields and others illegally scaling the Great Pyramids of Giza in Egypt for selfies and video content.
- **Dangerous experiences:** Tourists falling to their death off a cliff's edge or into boiling geysers whilst taking selfies in Yosemite National Park, United States. The popular "Train Street" in Hanoi, Vietnam was blocked off to tourists in 2019 due to selfie-seekers dodging trains and overcrowding on the tracks.
- **Culturally insensitive actions:** Bloggers setting up fashion photoshoots at religious sites, such as Fushimi Inari Shrine in Kyoto, Japan, or smiling selfies at Auschwitz, Poland.
- **Unrealistic expectations:** When the reality of the destination doesn't match expectations based on social media imagery. More on this under *Problems Faced by Tourists* in Part III.
- **Unethical animal selfies:** Tourists becoming injured by wild animals in the name of a photo, such as 200 selfie-related injuries from wild deer in Nara, Japan during 2018 and multiple injuries caused by bison in Yellowstone National Park, United States.

Glamourisation of a Travel Lifestyle

Adopting travel as an ongoing part of one's lifestyle became the hot new trend from around 2015 onwards. The rise of the travel "influencer" exploded with people chasing coveted sponsored hotel stays, paid social media posts and free activities at a given destination.

To cash in on the demand, many successful influencers felt the desire to coach others for a fee on how to quit their typical 9-5 jobs to be "digital nomads" - someone whose work can be done from anywhere in the world, provided they have an Internet connection. I mean, who wouldn't want to spend their working days on a laptop by a poolside in Bali?

Some people have wanted to show their online followers they lived a glamorous travel lifestyle so badly they snuck into business class cabins to post photos[21] of themselves in luxurious seats, when they actually paid for tickets to fly in economy. In extreme cases, they have even hired studio sets[22] made to look like inside private jets to stage their photos.

Creating the illusion that this sort of luxurious lifestyle is easily attainable can drive impressionable people to want to travel for the wrong reasons.

Features in Traditional Media

Media such as TV series, movies, music videos and the like have played a major role in influencing tourists' decisions to visit certain locations. The term "set jetters" (you may need to read that twice as I did at first) has been used to describe these die-hard fans keen to see places featured in their favourite shows, films and popular culture.

Specialised tours chauffeuring tourists around to filming hotspots and movie sets were created to meet demand, such as *Outlander* tours in Scotland and *Hobbiton* from *Lord of the Rings* in New Zealand to name a few.

There are countless examples I could list (and I'm sure you would have your own spring to mind), so here are a small handful to give you an idea of the measurable influence traditional media has had on tourism decisions:

- In Japan anime tourism[23] has existed since the early 1990's due to the popularity of the *Sailor Moon* cartoon series. However the term "anime pilgrimage" became widely used from 2008 to describe a set list of locations throughout the country favoured by anime-loving tourists.
- The mayor of Dubrovnik, Croatia, estimated that the popular TV series *Game of Thrones* was directly responsible for the city's 10% year-on-year tourism growth since the show began in 2011. Additionally, tourism was boosted by 15% in Seville, Spain in 2013 thanks to the series.
- Visitors to Fjadrargljufur Canyon in Iceland exploded - up to an 80% increase from 2016 and 2018 - according to the Environmental Agency of Iceland. The location appeared in Justin Beiber's *I'll Show You* music video in 2015.
- In 2019, the success of the HBO mini-series *Cherobyl* based on the 1986 nuclear disaster in Ukraine saw a whopping 40% increase in tours to the radioactive exclusion zone of Pripyat.

While I personally haven't solely visited a destination for the purpose of media tourism, I have to admit I've hunted down filming locations if I were visiting the area anyway - just ask my travel buddy how he begrudgingly allowed me to drag him around New York City in search of *Gossip Girl* or *Sex and the City* filming spots!

There are ways in which we can experience our favourite locations without contributing to overcrowding. You'll find out more in Part IV.

Overview: Part II

Hearing stories from distant, unfamiliar lands and undertaking lengthy journeys to experience them means modern-day tourists aren't too dissimilar to their ancestors who travelled for enjoyment. However in contemporary times, more people felt compelled to travel than ever before due to the amalgamation of a number of trends.

An oversaturation of information, technological advancements, commercialisation of mass tourism, glamourisation of a travel lifestyle and features in traditional media were on a collision course with travel becoming increasingly accessible and affordable. The outcome was overtourism and problems that come with it.

Before we can use our hidden power to its full potential, we need to learn from history so we are not doomed to repeat it. This involves understanding the negative impacts these trends have caused to help build our strategy in combating them.

PART III

PROBLEMS & NEGATIVE IMPACTS OF TOURISM

"If you are unable to understand the cause of a problem, it is impossible to solve it." - Naoto Kan.

Before I had ever sat on a donkey, I couldn't help but utter a slight giggle when I saw the rack of postcards in a Santorini souvenir store. A cartoon depicting a cruise ship arriving in the caldera caused a donkey to painfully exclaim "Oh, sh*t!". That was tourism on this Greek island, summed up on a colourful piece of cardboard.

While this was funny at first, soon after I realised the reality of this gimmicky postcard. The local donkeys carrying overweight tourists on their backs up 600 stairs from Fira's Old Town port very likely *do* exclaim such profanities in their heads.

In a perfect world, the aim of tourism should be for tourists to visit a destination, enjoy the country, its culture, and leave a positive impact. As we're familiar with by now, the complete opposite has occurred in countless cases as profits have been put above people.

Now we've unearthed the factors that contributed to the tourism boom from 2008, let's examine the cultural, economical and social problems that overwhelmed some of the world's most popular tourist destinations.

The Negative Impacts of Tourism

While tourism can bring benefits to local communities, it can also have unintended consequences. The negative impacts of tourism, especially mass tourism, can have a domino effect and contribute to the demise of a destination culturally, environmentally and financially. The following examples explain how.

i) The Loss of Cultural Identity & Community

A destination that experiences a loss of cultural identity is perhaps the biggest driving factor behind my passion to write this handbook. Some of the major reasons we enjoy travelling is the chance to experience different cultures, sights, cuisine and so much more. Each is special in their own unique way, and that's a beautiful thing deserving of protection.

But what happens when these destinations start to lose hold of their traditional ties and solely aim to appease visitors? The answer is a monocultural economy heavily dependent on tourism.

We should all ask ourselves this very important question: *What is the point of visiting a new destination if it just ends up being the same as everywhere else?*

Examples of destinations in danger of losing their cultural identity include:

- **Athens, Greece,** where whole residential neighbourhoods became tourist hotbeds. **Amsterdam, Netherlands,** where skyrocketing rents pushed locals out of the city in favour of UHA services, and even tourists began to complain[24] that they only saw other tourists.
- **Bali, Indonesia**, "Instagram tours" and smoothie bowls - unrelated to Balinese culture but popular with Western

tourists - became a staple for most foreign visitors.

- **Barcelona, Spain,** where everyday shops locals frequented were replaced[25] with souvenir stores, bike rental shops and expensive tourist-trap restaurants.
- **Gold Coast, Australia**, its main street once lined with good ol' pubs converted many into Chinese and Indian restaurants in response to the boom in new visitors from these countries (who aren't as fond of pub culture as the locals).
- **Lisbon, Portugal,** where it's claimed there were 9 restaurants on one street serving avocado on toast purely to attract tourists.
- **Vatican City**, where a Cardinal who opposed the opening of a global fast food franchise stated, "Over the last few years, the identity of this area has been lost[26]." More on this under *Loss of Authenticity* below.

There are dozens of similar situations, but by now I'm sure you can start to see the bigger picture.

In referencing the situation in Amsterdam, Responsible Travel[27] writes, "The streets feel less lived in… The homogenisation of the high street risks ruining the very character of the city that people come to experience in the first place."

ii) Loss of Authenticity, Erosion of Local Culture & Heritage

With its crumbled-façade buildings dating back to the 15th century, Vietnam's small coastal town of Hội An was listed as a UNESCO World Heritage site in 1999. This recognition combined with its picturesque Old Quarter, one of the best examples of preserved Southeast Asian trading ports from the time, helped to highlight Hội An on the tourist map.

In 2017, the small town saw 3.2 million tourists pass through its narrow streets and laneways much to the concern of its 120,000 local residents. 8,000 of the 10,000 daily visitors descended on the town from 3pm - 9pm, causing overcrowding. The replacement of local stores by shops and cafés specifically for tourists has pushed the town's inhabitants over to its outskirts. Perhaps this review on TripAdvisor by *Ozziewandera* succinctly sums it up:

> *"I was lucky enough to first visit Hội An in 2011 and found it to be amazing. Beautiful architecture, charming people and a quiet and laid back experience. On my second trip in April 2019 it was a completely different experience. Oppressively overcrowded with tour groups, many thousands of which are bussed into the city each night mostly to take photos for their social media. What was once a magical view of Vietnam now feels like an overcrowded shopping mall. The Old Town was once only a walking/bicycle area is now crowded with motorbikes and a constant cacophony of horns and engines. Streetwise touts harassing travellers to buy tailored suits and shoes at every corner. Stay away!"*

A loss of authenticity in tourism is when locals change for tourists rather than the other way around. Does being granted UNESCO World Heritage status help or hinder a destination?

While earning a UNESCO title supports heritage preservation of the place, it doesn't extend to the people who call it home - which is equally important. Is what we are seeing at these destinations "UNESCO-cide?"[28] Countless destinations have suffered a similar fate to Hội An after being granted UNESCO status.

The Guardian[29] states:

> *"Many of the 1,052 destinations across the world that have been stamped with United Nations world heritage status struggle to strike the balance between the economic benefits of catering to visitors and preserving the culture that drew the recognition."*

Throughout many articles on my blog, I argue that spending a short amount of time at any destination hinders the ability to scratch beneath the surface. With limited time, tourists all rush around to the same spots at the same time. How "authentic" and original is that sort of experience?

The loss of authenticity is a vicious cycle. Once granted UNESCO World Heritage status, a destination inevitably attracts more tourists. This in turn equals businesses catering to tourist needs and an increase in demand for UHA services. Commercialisation in this way can lead to the authenticity of the destination becoming heavily diluted.

Loss of authenticity also extends to the same multinational retail stores and fast food franchises gradually popping up in major destinations. This does not come without controversy, as some would argue fast food and fashion corporations are symbols of globalisation and mass consumerism - more on this under *Economic Leakage* coming up shortly.

Disputing these stores clash with the aesthetics of the surrounding centuries-old architecture, as previously mentioned the cardinals of Vatican City banded together in 2016 to protest against opening a global fast food franchise overlooking St Peter's Square!

Cardinal Elio Sgreccia stated, "[Opening the franchise was] by no means respectful of the architectural traditions of one of the most characteristic squares which look onto the colonnade of Saint Peters," along with the increase in illegal food stalls and souvenir stands selling cheap trinkets.

iii) Increased Pressure on Local Resources

As the tourism industry tends to be seasonal in nature, in some destinations it's calculated that there are more than ten times[30] the inhabitants in the high season than in the low season. The high demand during peak season can place enormous strain on local infrastructure such as:

- Water systems
- Roads
- Bridges
- Pathways
- Communication and energy systems (heating, cooling, etc)
- Mass transit systems and airports
- Sewerage.

When economic leakage comes into play, this can create major problems.

iv) Economic Leakage: Tourism Money Not Returning to Host Communities

As ecstatic as I was to arrive in Athens, my travel buddy and I were well aware that Greece had suffered greatly since the GFC. Despite being a popular tourist destination, money from visitors was not returning to local communities. Hopping into a taxi to take us to the city centre from the airport, our local Greek taxi driver wanted to practice his English so we gladly obliged.

Chatting with us about Greece's financial struggles one moment then about his wife and small children the next, he was so lovely we decided to privately hire his taxi services for a day during our time in Athens, allowing him to show us his favourite places the majority of tourists miss.

He drove us a scenic way alongside turquoise waters of the Athenian Riviera to Cape Sounion, where we explored the ancient Temple of Poseidon. Stopping at picturesque locations of his choosing on our return to Athens, we were taken aback by the beauty of emerald Lake Vouliagmeni, its geothermal waters believed to have healing powers by locals. We certainly would not have visited these locations nor felt a deeper connection to them without his knowledge. By the end of the day as we said our goodbyes, all three of us were grateful for our fulfilling encounter.

When money is not returned to local communities, it becomes a major problem in tourism. Money leaving the host country to be filtered back elsewhere is known as *economic leakage* in tourism. While the host destination hopes to make money from tourism and welcomes foreign entities with open arms, very little can actually end up back in their hands to benefit local communities.

Entities that contribute to economic leakage in tourism are:

- **Large international tour group companies**
  Usually based in the UK or US, companies providing large group tours (around 50 people) in Asia or Europe are cost effective for tourists. However, these companies usually employ foreign tour guides who may not have as much knowledge about the destination as local people. These tours focus on the common places and whisk the group around to many popular spots within a short timeframe, with little time for visitors to explore on their own terms and spend money locally. Profit from these tours goes back to the company in the UK or US rather than the local host community.

- **Large cruises**
  Mega cruise ship vacations are popular for tourists travelling on a budget. Everything has been provided, where tourists sleep, eat most meals and enjoy entertainment on board. In turn, the local communities these cruises visit receive little money towards the issues that arise from hosting tourists throughout the day.

- **Large international hotel chains**
  Internationally recognised hotel chains are favourites of

tourists who like to cash in points towards their stays at a destination. Large international hotel chains employ foreigners familiar with Western customs and speak English, sometimes overlooking locals. Money from these stays goes back to the parent company offshore.

- **Multinational fast food and fast fashion corporations**
  Huge fast food and fast fashion corporations offer safety in familiarity for tourists. Visitors flock to these recognisable brands because they know what to expect, instead of supporting small locally run businesses. Money spent at these fast food and fast fashion chains doesn't stay long in the local economy before it gets passed higher up the chain (and offshore). The fast-paced nature of these brands often leads to an impersonal customer service experience.

The Italian city of Venice is the perfect example of where economic leakage has caused immense problems. Prior to 2020, up to 70,000 visitors from outside town would flock into Venice each day. Statistics showed that out of 26 million people who visited Venice annually, only 50% actually spent the night in local accommodation. This is a major missed opportunity for the local economy and communities who live in the 1,600 year-old floating city.

What's more telling is the correlation between the number of locals leaving Venice and the increase of tourism to the city. During 1931, Venice was home to 164,000 local residents. Today, that number has shrunk by almost two-thirds to 55,000.

v) Overcrowding & Vehicle Traffic Congestion

Whilst I tried my darndest to admire the Mars Room in the Château de Versailles, it was a very unfulfilling experience. It had nothing to do with the intricate beauty and history of the red room itself; the major issue being I was shuffling through at a snail's space amongst a mosh-pit of tourists. No time to stop and admire details when there's a horde of sweaty and disgruntled tourists pressing on you from all sides. It became less about what I was there to see and more about trying not to get crushed.

I couldn't help but think the room felt beyond capacity, unable to be enjoyed or appreciated in the way it deserved considering the Château's lifespan of four centuries in France. My thoughts were abruptly interrupted by a tourist's scream. The English word "THIEF" suddenly bellowed through the white noise, as one tourist accused another of pickpocketing them. I mean, we were all squeezed so closely together in that room, it was impossible to not be touching anyone else.

Tightly gripping my small crossbody bag towards my front, I couldn't help but think about what the walls of that room would say if given the ability to speak. I'm sure they would have been reduced to tears when describing the uncapped cash-grab France's former royal court had become.

It's no secret that an increase in visitors to a city will ultimately lead to traffic congestion in both human and vehicle form. Footpaths become so overcrowded it's difficult for local workers to navigate their own cities, while residents are forced to wait in lengthy traffic jams due to peak season visitors loading onto tour buses.

Prior to 2020, here are some examples of cities who became fed up with various types of tourism congestion and their proposals to help bring it under control:

- **Barcelona, Spain** banned Segways and scooters from its Old Town and beachfront footpaths.
- **Dubrovnik, Croatia** became so overcrowded it risked losing its UNESCO world heritage status. The mayor urged to cap daily visitors[31] to 4,000 after UNESCO suggested reducing numbers to 8,000.

- **Paris, France** banned tourist buses from the city centre in July 2019. Paris' deputy mayor, Emmanuel Grégoire, claimed the increasing number of tourist buses contributed to overcrowding, traffic congestion, noise and air pollution.
- **Prague, Czech Republic** banned electric Limebikes, scooters and Segways in its cobbled Old Town.
- **Santorini, Greece** wanted to minimise its cruise ship visitors from 12,000 to 8,000 per day.

In an extreme example, **Venice, Italy** hoped to cap daily visitors to 70,000 so they wouldn't greatly outnumber the 55,000 local residents. In an effort to divert day-tripping tourists away from popular areas, the city trialled a weekend of controversial turnstile gates to segregate locals from visitors in May 2018.

The measure was not well received by local residents nor the tourism industry, with protesters creating "This is not Veniceland" signs. Tommaso Cacciari, of *Comitato No Grandi Navi* (No Grand Ships) shared an interesting perspective on the situation:

> "This is the worst initiative imaginable, which does nothing to solve our tourism problem. Mass tourism has destroyed this city in the last 10 years... The real problem is that the politicians who run this city want to turn it into a theme park. So these metal barriers are not to limit access but the opposite: to show that our home is already a museum and entertainment park. It announces to the world that, like Disneyland, Venice opens and closes with a gate."

Similarly, Responsible Travel's[32] CEO, Justin Francis quoted:

> "Now we end up with segregation of tourists and local people. It seems it's now official that Venice has been reduced to a theme park. Tourism is about bringing people together, residents and visitors, and when done

properly, both parties should reap the benefits. It should never be about segregation."

vi) Dependence on Tourism

While it's always been important for countries to have a diverse range of industries contributing to the health of their economies and Gross Domestic Product (GDP), the events of 2020 certainly highlighted this essential requirement more than ever before. Unfortunately for some countries, this isn't entirely possible and tourism contributes to an overwhelmingly high percentage of jobs in the industry as well as to their GDP.

A local economy that relies heavily on tourism as its primary source of income is going to be a fickle one, vulnerable to factors beyond its control such as natural disasters, terrorism, political changes or health epidemics. Tourism to Nepal reduced by one-third after the major 2015 earthquake, and tourists stopped coming to the ancient Pyramids of Giza altogether in 2011 due to political unrest in Egypt.

As most of us have now seen first-hand to an extent, without tourism many sectors suffer such as hotels, retail, local tour companies and the like. Locals don't necessarily indulge in these kinds of activities and experiences day-to-day, leaving a huge void in income for those working in these fields.

Small island nations particularly have a high dependence on tourism, which can have detrimental effects when the focus shifts from prioritising the needs of local citizens to making tourists happy. As locals begin to move away, an overdependence on tourism can result in overtourism issues. It's another vicious cycle, isn't it?

To give you an overall idea of countries and their dependence on tourism, the following figures[33] represent the percentage in contribution of travel and tourism to each country's GDP (as a share of GDP):

•	Macau	72%	• Thailand	21%
•	Maldives	66%	• Greece	21%
•	Grenada	55%	• Portugal	19%
•	Vanuatu	48%	• New Zealand	18%
•	Belize	44%	• Mexico	17%
•	Bahamas	40%	• Spain	14%
•	Fiji	40%	• Italy	13%
•	Jamaica	34%	• Egypt	12%
•	Iceland	33%	• United Kingdom	10%
•	Croatia	25%	• Australia	10%

Source: Knoema.com

When speaking about Venice, Italy, Tommaso Cacciari of *Comitato No Grandi Navi* (No Grand Ships) quoted, "Rather than stupid turnstiles and police checks, we need housing that allows Venetians to live in their city, rather than tourist B&Bs, and an economy that is diverse rather than solely about tourism."

vii) Destruction of Historical Monuments & Environment

This is one of the most depressing tourism problems. Some of the main reasons we travel is to see incredible monuments from centuries past and breathtaking natural scenery. But what happens when tourists begin to destroy things they came to see - whether intentional or not?

Here are some examples of destruction to historical monuments and the environment caused by tourism:

- **Angkor Wat, Cambodia:** Over 7,000 daily tourists trampled the famous lakeside overlooking the ancient temple to watch the sunrise. The visitor boom also increased demand on local water supplies, forcing authorities to access groundwater. This action lowered the water table[34] and has potential to cause the temples built on it to destabilise.

- **Cairo, Egypt:** A 3,500 year old Egyptian stone carving was vandalised by a 12 year old tourist scrawling his name on it.
- **Kyoto, Japan:** Tourists etched their names into the delicate green stems of Arashiyama Bamboo Grove, a UNESCO World Heritage site. Tourists from large tour groups have also been known to steal[35] religious talismans from temples.
- **Lisbon, Portugal:** Damage to local buildings caused by theft[36] of traditional *azujelo* tiles, sold illegally and fetching hundreds of Euros per piece in antique stores.
- **Maya Bay, Thailand:** Popularly known as James Bond Island, the bay was closed to tourists in 2018 as a result of litter, water pollution and damage to local reefs caused by day-tripping boats from neighbouring Phuket and Krabi.
- **Paris, France:** Destruction to the 200-year old Pont des Arts bridge caused by love locks attached by tourists. In 2015, an entire section of the bridge collapsed and fell into the River Seine below.
- **Prague, Czech Republic:** Padlocks near Charles Bridge were removed by authorities to prevent rust and decay to the structure. It's been calculated that 13.2 tonnes of padlocks have been removed from this spot since 2009.
- **Reykjadalur, Iceland:** Extreme damage to fragile soil from tourists wandering off pathways resulted in the area along with Fjarðárgljúfur Canyon and Skógaheið being closed to tourists in 2018 to allow the muddy grounds to rejuvenate.
- **Southern California, USA:** In spring 2019, social media influencers were blamed for the destruction of rare poppy fields by trampling flowers when wandering off marked paths, crushing flowers by laying in them and picking flowers to take photos. Some seeds were waiting under the soil for decades for the right conditions to bloom.

You can help by calling out bad behaviour as you see it so people who are ignorant or malicious think twice about their actions. More examples of the wider environmental impacts can be found in the Further Reading section at the end of this book.

viii) Animal Exploitation

Animal exploitation has been a huge negative consequence of mass tourism. I've seen first-hand how the donkeys of Santorini were abused into carrying overweight tourists up a cliffside, had friends who petted chained tigers and rode elephants in Thailand, and knew many tourists who visited exotic animal cafés throughout Japan. There was once a time where these kinds of activities were considered acceptable.

It can be a sensitive topic as animals can form part of a destination's local cultural heritage. Some animals have worked alongside and benefited humans for centuries, so while it may no longer be acceptable through today's eyes, it's important to understand why animals may have been used in this way. That's not to say we should allow exploitation to continue, though!

Although many of us, as well as myself, have undertaken some animal experiences in the past before knowing any unintended consequences, since then I've personally never recommended animal experiences to my readers because of some unpopular truths I learnt over the years. We never *really* know what can go on behind the scenes once tourists have gone for the day.

Some negative consequences of animals being forced to work in terrible conditions for the purpose of tourism were:

- **Selfies with chained tigers in Thailand**
  It was revealed[37] these animals were drugged and declawed. Tiger cubs were separated from their mothers just 3 weeks after birth, while more mature tigers had also been starved as punishment for "bad" behaviour as well as provided no

access to fresh drinking water.

- **Elephant "sanctuaries" across Thailand** that claimed to be ethical, however it was found the animals were forced to wade in waters for lengthy periods and interact with tourists.
- **Riding camels in the desert in Africa and the Middle East** Many short camel rides in a day meant the camels didn't get the chance to properly rest between each, leaving them fatigued. Longer rides are thought to be more beneficial for the animal as they get the chance to rest properly when riders do throughout the day.
- **Wild animal cafés and villages in Japan** Nocturnal animals such as owls and hedgehogs were forced to be awake during the day and handled by people in Tokyo cafés. Foxes are solitary creatures in the wild, but are still crammed together, caged and fight each other for food at the Miyagi Zao Fox Village in Sendai.
- **Zonkeys in Mexico** Especially in Tijuana, locals have painted donkeys with black and white zebra stripes, hence the name "zonkey". The animal is then tied up to a Mexico-themed backdrop whilst wearing decorative headpieces to attract tourist money from photos.
- **Travelling circuses and performances** Wild animals are trained to perform tricks for an audience. According to PETA[38], an investigation found exotic animals such as elephants, lions and tigers were forced into training by being whipped, muzzled and even tasered into compliance. They're also confined in small spaces for lengthy periods when being transported to the next location, sometimes without adequate food or access to water.
- **Zoo experiences** Where wild animals are kept in dreadful, unnatural living conditions. Examples include concrete rooms for kangaroos in Shanghai Zoo, China. A kangaroo was stoned to death[39] in its enclosure by visitors as they were attempting to make it hop in Fuzhou, China.

- **Aquariums where dolphins and whales are kept in captivity**
As whales and dolphins use echolocation in the wild, in captivity their reverberations bounce off the walls of their small enclosures and can drive them insane[40]. The Netflix documentary *Blackfish* released in 2013 is said to have played a role in raising awareness of killer whales' plight in captivity.

iv) Increased Prices on Goods & Services

On our last afternoon in the old city of Kuşadası, Turkey, my partner and I went in search of bottled water to purchase. In an area of town that was not busy, we stumbled across a kiosk selling 2 litre bottles with no prices displayed. When asking the store owner the price for one, he quite literally looked us up and down, paused, then proclaimed "€4" in a confident tone.

Knowing that was obviously his "tourist" price, we shook our heads and said we'd give him €4 for two bottles, to which he agreed. Despite Turkey's national currency being the Lira (not the Euro which has a higher value), the store owner had likely charged unsuspecting tourists this overinflated price many times before.

Once a destination begins to depend more on tourism, it can lead to a price increase on goods and services. A British family visiting Rome, Italy in 2013 made international headlines when they were charged €64 for four gelato[41], prompting an apology from the mayor and multiple complaints to local authorities about tourists being unfairly overcharged. Always check before purchasing!

An increase in tourism can hike prices up not just for tourists who can be accustomed to (or unaware of) paying more anyway, but for locals who need to live and work at the destination, too. Tourism ends up competing with local residents for the best accommodation, food, attractions and transport the destination has to offer.

As investment property owners began to realise they could make more money by renting out whole apartments to short-term tourists than local residents, housing prices skyrocketed in cities popular with UHA. Income for local residents did not increase at the same rate, resulting in many becoming priced out of their own cities such as Barcelona, Venice and Dublin.

x) Increased Pollution in Different Forms

An increase in tourism activities inevitably leads to an increase in pollution. Examples of pollution caused by tourism include, but certainly aren't limited to, the following:

Water pollution

- **Spain:** Due to being home to some of the world's largest cruise ships, Barcelona earnt itself the undesirable title of the most polluted port in Europe[42].
- **Globally:** Foe.org reports cruise ships collectively dumped one billion gallons[43] of sewage into the oceans in 2014. Much of this was untreated, containing heavy metals and other types of contaminants.
- **Italy:** Seabed erosion[44] in Venice's lagoon due to oversized cruise ships passing through and stirring up sediments.

Air pollution

- **Globally:** Tour buses are left running whilst tourists are out, so they can return to cool air conditioning. This creates toxic fumes and smog.
- **Globally:** Cruise ships burn unrefined crude oil when cruising and whilst docked at port to create electricity for crew and passengers, creating toxic fumes and smog. Furthermore The New York Times[45] reported cruise ships

can emit 3 to 4 times the amount of carbon dioxide per passenger mile than a jet.

- **Globally:** Burning of fuel from aircraft, most of which is used for takeoff and landing, contributing to 2% of global carbon (CO_2) emissions.

Noise pollution

- **Italy:** Oversized cruise ships mooring, creating vibrations that rattle the fragile buildings in Venice.
- **Greece:** Tourists chatting loudly on their phones at important sacred sites such as the Acropolis of Athens.
- **Globally:** Tourists flying noisy drones without local permits and disrupting residents and wildlife.
- **Globally:** Constant engine sounds from planes, cars, buses and even snowmobiles for tourism purposes.
- **Globally:** Entertainment noise from outdoor performances held for tourists.

Other kinds of pollution

- **Littering of solid waste:** Not only ruins natural scenery but can pollute waterways if not disposed of correctly. In 2019, 11,000 kilograms of rubbish was collected and removed from the Nepalese side of Mount Everest.
- **Tourist pollution:** Overtourism became unbearable in Kyoto, Japan, leading the locals to coin a new phrase, *kankō kōgai* (tourist pollution) to describe visitor crowds.

xi) Issues with Voluntourism

Voluntourism, short for "volunteer tourism," is a rising trend amongst young people wanting to meaningfully contribute to communities primarily across South-East Asia, Africa and Latin America. These types of volunteer holidays abroad can include teaching, community support, youth development, animal and environmental conservation in developing countries.

It's now possible to book all-inclusive voluntourism package tours, much the same as booking a cruise or resort-style holiday. According to Save The Children[46], voluntourists can pay up to USD $1,500 per week to spend their time assisting local communities, contributing to an industry that is worth USD $1.97 billion per year.

During 2018, voluntourism holidays increased by 33% on the previous year. Well-meaning tourists usually have their hearts in the right place, however there is a dark side to this form of tourism. Regrettably, the saying "the road to hell is paved with good intentions" comes to mind.

Criticisms of Voluntourism

When researching examples and criticisms of voluntourism, I tripped and fell down a rabbit hole of information - a rabbit hole I never imagined would be so deep and dark.

I'll cover just a few examples as this topic can involve children and become quite sensitive. If you would like to research more about what happens when tourists aren't around, there are a wealth of interviews, data and articles to be found online and in the Further Reading section at the end of this book.

Criticisms of voluntourism include:
- Unskilled volunteers can replace skilled local workers in areas where unemployment is already high.
- Short-term projects for volunteers can mean limited time to work on them, not benefiting local host communities in the long-term.
- Volunteers without qualifications or experience have unsupervised contact with vulnerable children.
- Inconsistent short-term attachments formed by children with volunteers can lead to separation anxiety and damage their mental health.
- Volunteers' money goes towards making their experience

comfortable rather than going to disadvantaged people in the local host community.
- Some people may volunteer for the wrong reasons: Do it just to include on their CV to compete with job candidates or as an excuse to delay tertiary studies.

Having been a global trailblazer raising awareness to the problems with voluntourism before they were widely recognised, Daniela Papi, founder of Cambodian aid organisation PEPY[47], explains "Any orphanage that will let you in off the street without requiring background checks or without requiring that you are qualified for a specific role is not one at which you should be volunteering."

To sum up issues with voluntourism, one could reference the quote by Chinese philosopher Lao Tzu: *"Give a man a fish and you feed him for a day. Teach a man to fish and you feed him for a lifetime."*

Child Exploitation

Like countless industries, voluntourism with children is big business. According to a report by The Guardian[48] in 2018, despite the Khmer Rouge genocide in Cambodia over 40 years ago, the number of orphanages was growing. This was due to an increase in Australian tourists paying big money to volunteer there, not a rise in abandoned children.

A 2016 study by Lumos found out of 32,000 children in orphanages in Haiti, 80% were not actual orphans and either had one or both parents still alive.

In order for the money to continue to stream into some unethical orphanages, they need "orphans" and can exploit struggling local parents to hand over their children with the promise of access to food, education, healthcare and other special services.

In extreme cases, a child can be sold for adoption to parents in wealthy countries, known as *child laundering*. An Australian Parliamentary inquiry[49] details witness accounts of the cruel conditions and modern slavery children were forced to endure in a Cambodian orphanage.

It could be argued some forms of voluntourism don't actually put the needs of the local community first, running these kinds of projects with little to no input from the people they claim to support.

Exploiting children for profit is absolutely heartbreaking. If voluntourism is something you hope to experience someday, I kindly ask you to thoroughly research reputable companies, dig deeper into how the children are treated and follow the money where possible.

By now I hope it's starting to become clear that our demands as tourists are the power that can forcefully drive change. Remember, the industry caters to us.

Problems Faced by Tourists

It's not just locals who face issues from tourism. Although the benefits of travelling can be numerous for tourists, that's not to say it's always smooth sailing. Tourists also face problems that can ruin the experience they spent months (or even years) saving up their hard-earned money to enjoy.

Many negative impacts of tourism can be prevented with a little prior planning and understanding ahead of time, which we'll explore in detail in Part IV.

In an effort to promote the glamorous sides of travel, photos shared across social media from popular destinations seldom show problems faced by tourists. The following are just a few examples.

i) Overtourism

According to the Oxford dictionary, *overtourism* can be defined as "the phenomenon whereby certain places of interest are visited by excessive numbers of tourists, causing undesirable effects for the places visited."

We all hope to have memorable travel experiences for the right reasons, however overtourism can hinder our best efforts. It increases competition amongst tourists for the best accommodation, the strain it places on local transport, the time needed to book activities and restaurants in advance. Not to mention having to fight it out to take photos of popular landmarks or attractions without crowds of people in them.

ii) Disappointment Due to Unrealistic Expectations

"Oh wow," I exclaimed when scrolling through Pinterest's search results for Scotland. "This place looks right out of a fantasy novel!" Beneath jagged mountain peaks, multiple cascading waterfalls fed into a shallow, crystal clear pool surrounded by mossy green boulders and small purple flowers. The waters were so clear, various sized stones were visible beneath the shallows. My travel buddy and I were planning to visit the Isle of Skye anyway, so the Fairy Pools of Glenbrittle would make a lovely little addition to our trip.

On the day of visiting, we became a little lost in our hire car as there was no signage to the Fairy Pools. Stopping off at a nearby pub, we asked a local for directions. "The Fairy Pools?" she questioned, "That sounds like a name made up for tourists as we don't know of anything by that name." She continued to provide us with directions to where we thought the pools were, which were easy to follow.

When arriving at the car park, the weather took a dreadful turn. Through blustering winds and horizontal rains, we battled a muddy path that seemed to go on forever before reaching a section of the adjacent stream that opened out into murky grey waters of what we could only think were the evasive Fairy Pools. Low-hanging clouds turned what would have been the mountainous backdrop into a grey haze.

"What? This is it?!" I yelled to my travel buddy over the sounds of relentless wind and rain. "It looks NOTHING like that photo!" he laughed hysterically, voice straining over the gale winds, "I told you this was a bad idea!" The walk back to the car through the sodden mud was much worse, though we couldn't help but realise we had learnt something from the ordeal.

You may have seen the TikTok trend *Instagram vs Reality* where tourists post an image of what they expect to see at their destination (hint: crowd-free, flawless photos) versus what they actually encountered there? Well, this is exactly the kind of thing I mean when I talk about tourists setting unrealistic expectations.

Perception is reality, right? When browsing Instagram or Pinterest for inspiration for your next trip, you'll likely see an array of picture-perfect, heavily edited images. If everyone has them, that must be what you can expect, too? What they don't show is people squeezing past each other on busy footpaths, piles of rubbish left strewn on the streets or even the stench of sewerage.

One perfect example of unrealistic expectations can be found at the Gates of Heaven in Bali, Indonesia. Photos on social media present this temple as two oversized stone monoliths with reflective waters in front. Instagrammers would line up for hours to get a coveted photo at this iconic spot, only to be disappointed to learn the mirrored water was actually an illusion created by an iPhone trick[50].

It surprises me that these people didn't research the spot they were visiting in more detail, as the omission of the waters would be bleedingly obvious if they'd checked outside social media. It only proves visiting a location for the sole purpose of a photo is not a meaningful travel experience!

iii) Long Wait Times Due to Social Media Popularity

Uniformly sitting in a snow covered valley of the Japanese Alps lies the 19th century village of Shirakawa-go. Dotted with grassho-thatched wooden townhouses coated in layers of snow against a mountainous backdrop, it's no wonder this location is high on most tourists' Japan wishlist.

However, something that is not mentioned in tourist guide books or blogs is what goes on behind-the-scenes of photos from this idyllic winter wonderland. To capture the iconic shot above the village from the dedicated viewpoint, visitors need to queue up in freezing cold conditions for over two hours.

Shirakawa-go is one glaring example of the problems that tourists face at popular destinations. Getting that sought-after picture has arguably made travel more competitive in nature. For many it seems to have become about checking places off a list and achieving the same shots as everyone else. Do you agree?

iv) Flight Shaming

Known as *flygskam* in Sweden where the term was founded, the flight shaming movement began in 2018. Its aim is to encourage the reduction of aviation's impact on the environment by promoting more eco-friendly overland transport alternatives such as high-speed trains.

Not only are trains a greener option, they can be a more efficient use of travel time for short distances because there's no need to go through the lengthy process of checking a bag, going through airport security, boarding, or take-off and landing. Teenage climate activist Greta Thunburg became the face of the movement, which grew in popularity across Northern Europe before making global headlines. While flight shaming made some travellers hesitant towards flying, a 2019 Honeywell Aerospace report[51] found private jets emit up to 40 times as much carbon dioxide per passenger than their commercial counterparts.

In response to flight shaming, the Swedish term *att smygflyga* or "flying in secret" was coined to describe people who travelled by plane without revealing it to others over fears of receiving negative attention.

Flight shaming is not a one-size-fits-all solution. In larger countries such as the United States with limited long-distance rail networks, not flying can be difficult to justify. The same can be said for island countries such as my homeland of Australia and neighbouring New Zealand, where flying in our modern age is the more obvious choice than spending months stowed away on some sort of shipping vessel.

v) Greenwashing

Have you heard of *greenwashing*? This term is used to describe establishments such as hotels or tour companies that claim they are environmentally friendly but have no formal certifications to back it up. They may use terminology such as *eco-friendly* and display green leaf logos, but this can be misleading to tourists.

Well-meaning tourists who support these companies can cause more harm than good without realising. Some examples of greenwashing include:

- Wildlife attractions that offer animal shows or allow

tourists to closely interact with the animals. Genuine wildlife sanctuaries won't do this.

- Wildlife tours that allow tourists to feed wild animals as this disturbs the animals' natural behaviours.
- Local tours that claim to support their community but offer visits to orphanages, or push tourists to purchase unethical souvenirs such as exotic animal skins.
- Accommodation providers who claim they are eco-friendly but don't have a sustainability policy in place, or launder towels anyway even after they've been hung for re-use.
- Eco-tour operators that can't explain why their tours have a low impact on the environment. Operating in the environment doesn't necessarily mean *eco-friendly*.

More examples of greenwashing can be found at EcoTravelist[52]. You can help call out these kinds of issues by politely addressing the organisation's management to drive positive change.

vi) Increase in Animosity

In cities popular with tourists across the globe, mass tourism can lead to tension, hostility and resentment of visitors. With "Tourists Go Home" graffiti scrawled on across walls in Barcelona, Venice and Paris, you can't really blame locals for animosity against an overwhelming number of people who act in a disrespectful way towards them.

Sure, it's definitely not all tourists who misbehave! Unfortunately, the reality is the majority can make the minority look bad.

Locals have been annoyed by tourists when they...

- **Haven't made any effort** to learn a few phrases from the local language and expect everyone to speak English. It's considered rude anywhere.
- **Stuck to eating at touristy places** and major international

chains instead of supporting locally-run small businesses.

- **Clambered over residents' rooftops** and sent noisy drones flying in Oia, Santorini to capture the sunset.
- **Dawdled across multiple bike, tram and car lanes** on busy roads in Amsterdam.
- **Used quiet residential streets** such as Rue Crémieux in Paris to spend hours filming noisy music videos and disruptive photoshoots for social media campaigns.
- **Spread out in large group tours** hogging footpaths, blocking essential pathways, staircases and storefronts.
- **Lugged huge suitcases on public transport** during peak hour, taking up loads of space and bumping into other passengers.
- **Left rubbish** and mess behind at beaches, parks and forests.
- **Took Segway tours around busy cobbled streets** and discarded free electric scooters thoughtlessly in Prague, Czech Republic.
- **Took disrespectful photos and selfies** at culturally sensitive locations such as Auschwitz, Poland.
- **Headed into oncoming traffic** to take photos on Paris's iconic street, the Champs-Élysées.
- **Spoke loudly in otherwise quiet establishments** or areas of respect (such as temples or churches) in popular tourist destinations globally.
- **Took up all the capacity** of Tram 28 in Lisbon making it impossible for locals to use for their work commute.
- **Exploited free bus services** supposed to be for residents from their hillside homes down to local markets in Positano, Italy.
- **Set out hiking in flip-flops** and were ill-equipped for the terrain, having to be rescued by local helicopters in Cinque Terre, Italy.
- **Broke into hire cars** in New Zealand in search of other tourists' valuables.

This list could go on and on, but by now I'm sure you get the idea. It's these kinds of actions that give tourists a bad name.

vii) Targeted by Scams & Pickpockets

"Excuse me!" a shadowy figure called out in English as he hurried after my travel buddy on a main street in Paris. "Ignore it," I mentioned under my breath to my buddy, pulling her along despite her curiosity. I'd seen this before. "I think you dropped this," the figure insisted, holding out a gold ring in the palm of his hand on approach. Before she could examine the ring any closer, I yelled *"NON"* (the French word for "no") as I yanked my buddy away, walking briskly from the scene.

"But why?" she asked in confusion as the figure slinked off to wait for more unsuspecting passers-by. "It's a scam," I replied, "They pretend to find a ring on the street and attempt to either sell it to you or have an accomplice nearby to pickpocket you while you're distracted." "Ohhhh, thanks!" she sighed in relief, having just avoided a potentially unfortunate situation.

It isn't always tourists who do the wrong thing. Throughout many destinations around the world, pickpockets and scammers can be rife in areas popular with visitors. More people means more opportunities to commit crimes, and using crowds to their advantage allows them to get away undetected.

Tourists can be viewed as wealthy, often distracted and easier to target than locals, making obvious visitors sitting ducks for pickpockets. Combining these facts with overcrowding, it can create the perfect storm of conditions for something to go wrong for visitors.

Overview: Part III

Like the donkeys in Santorini seeing cruise ships approaching on the horizon, we've now had the chance to examine the problems and negative impacts of tourism. Destinations catering to tourists more than their own local residents has resulted in losses of culture, community and authenticity. Overcrowding has led to pressure on local resources, increases in prices and pollution in different forms.

A dependence on tourism can lead to economic leakage, while swathes of visitors can unintentionally contribute to damage to historical monuments, nature, animals and even local children.

Not only do locals face issues, tourists are confronted with their own set of complications. Dealing with animosity from locals, becoming targets for pickpockets and setting unrealistic expectations from the start can result in unfulfilling travel experiences and disappointment - none of which is ideal.

Now we know the causes behind the above problems, what solutions are there to minimise the negative social, cultural and economical impacts of overtourism for everyone?

PART IV

SOLUTIONS TO OVERTOURISM: HOW TO BE AN INVISIBLE TOURIST

"Sometimes the easiest way to solve a problem is to stop participating in the problem." - Jonathan Mead.

"So you're spending 9 days with us here in Barcelona?" the hotel's reception asked me to confirm. "Absolutely," I replied excitedly, eager to drop off my luggage and hit the streets to leave no stone unturned in Antoni Gaudí's living masterpiece outside. "This is a long time for most tourists," he added, to which I replied "I know, but there is just so much to see!"

After dreaming of visiting La Sagrada Família since I first laid eyes on it in Graham Hopwood's *Handbook of Art* textbook as a young girl, I knew I wanted to stay as long as possible to fully immerse myself in the city this elaborate and unfinished basilica called home.

I desired to get lost amongst Gaudí's architecture, learn why his basilica has been under construction since 1882, uncover his inspirations and do my own little self-guided Art Nouveau walking tour of unique buildings I had researched. I could barely wait to get started!

While I realise not everyone may have the luxury of choosing to stay in a city for 9 days as I did, I strongly recommend spending as long as your leave from work will allow to experience any destination to its fullest extent as a short-term visitor. But how do you determine how many nights to stay to achieve this?

You're about to learn the exact blueprint I always follow to ensure I minimise my tourist footprint and maximise my travel experiences in any given destination. My strategy has been carefully crafted over a decade through much trial and error, and now I'm about to share it all with you.

Are you ready to find out how you can become an Invisible Tourist before, during and even after a trip, too?

Get ready to begin tailoring your invisibility cloak - here we go!

BEFORE A TRIP

Blueprint for Planning a Stress-Free Travel Experience

In travel forums for Japan, I would often see visitors return from the country saying they'd had a great time, but were exhausted from squeezing too much into each day and rushing around in order to check off the items on their wishlists. Does that sound like you? No, no, no my friend. Don't make this critical mistake - you don't want to return from a holiday needing another to recover from the first!

I'll admit my process for planning a stress-free trip does take quite a bit of research upfront. But try to look at it this way: Would you rather plan and research before a trip than waste precious travel time trying to figure it all out once you're at the destination? That's time you won't ever get back and would be more wisely spent having fun.

In his wisdom Benjamin Franklin once said, "By failing to prepare, you are preparing to fail." Armed with my blueprint for planning the perfect travel itinerary, you'll be guaranteed to have the most enjoyable trip possible.

When referring to hotels throughout this chapter, I also mean regulated accommodation such as serviced apartments, traditional B&Bs, motels and the like. With that cleared up, let's begin!

Where Possible, Travel During Off-Peak Periods (Seasonally & Daily)

When are you planning to go? Travelling during off-peak times is one of my favourite overtourism solutions. If you're able to plan your travels during the off-season (shoulder season) it has many benefits. Not only is this a great way to save a little money for yourself, but also brings tourism money to locals at times when they actually need it.

Visiting Paris in March[53] is the perfect example. Hotels and flights cost less and crowds are also much smaller during this time. It's a win-win and one of the most important solutions to overtourism!

To find out when the off peak season is, type your destination and "shoulder season" into a search engine to bring up the answer. Official tourism websites for each country also provide useful advice for what to expect at different times of the year.

By travelling during off-peak periods, I'm also talking about daily as well as seasonally. As mentioned earlier, if you have suitcases try to avoid catching public transport during rush hour where commuters are already fighting it out to get to and from work.

If it's possible, you can also try to avoid travelling during major public holidays where crowds are already expected to be huge, like if you're planning a trip to Japan[54] around Golden Week, for instance.

Places like Barcelona, Lisbon, Venice and Santorini have been bombarded with cruise ships and day-trippers throughout summer in recent years, causing massive crowds and major overtourism issues. Local's lives have been negatively affected at an unsustainable rate.

Sure, the weather may not be as desirable for travelling during the off season, and you may need to deal with dreary weather, extra clothing and snow in some locations (but the weather can also surprise you, like it did during my week in Switzerland[55] during winter!). But that sure beats having to navigate through overcrowded areas and narrow cobbled streets, right?

TIP: It's understandable not everyone will have the ability to choose exactly what time of the year they travel due to employment commitments. In that case, you can implement navigating around during-off peak periods on a daily basis during your trip to improve your experience.

How to Determine the Length of an Upcoming Stay

When deciding on the length of stay at an upcoming destination, you'll need to reverse engineer the trip. But don't worry, this is not as difficult as it sounds! By following these steps, it's a piece of cake.

i) Create a wishlist

Firstly, note all the attractions you hope to see at the destination. You can find them featured in guide books, travel blogs like mine, or see what travellers are suggesting and reviewing over on TripAdvisor. Do you have a friend who has previously visited and can recommend an amazing spot you shouldn't miss?

ii) Visually arrange the wishlist on a map

You may wish to use something like Google My Maps to pinpoint these attractions visually on a map to analyse their locations in relation to one another. Or if you prefer the old school way, on a printed map. Group together attractions that are nearby to efficiently plan their visits on the same day to avoid backtracking.

TIP: The Google My Maps app (not to be confused with regular Google Maps) allows you to download your map for use offline. When at your destination, you can enable GPS tracking on the offline map without being charged for data.

iii) Calculate distances and times

Work out the time it takes to travel between each attraction on your wishlist. As an example, this can be done in Google Maps by typing in "Eiffel Tower to the Louvre" for it to pull up the travel time by foot, train or road. To this, add roughly how long you would ideally spend in each place. For iconic monuments this may be half an hour, while museums and art galleries may need 2-4 hours (sometimes more) to explore properly.

TIP: If the destination is popular with day-trippers, it may have previously suffered (or be vulnerable to) issues caused by overtourism. Plan to stay longer at these locations instead - more on this later.

iv) Don't forget time to relax!

I urge you to remember this very important thing: Plotting your trip to the minute, overplanning and being overly ambitious by squeezing too much into each day can become restrictive and exhausting. Things may not always go to plan and you'll have to go with the flow, so give yourself breathing room between activities and be realistic about how much you can see each day.

While being prepared is one of the best ways to avoid disappointment when travelling, overplanning doesn't work well for those who prefer being spontaneous. Becoming an Invisible Tourist is about embracing a balance between the two. Make sure to include some down time throughout your trip to allow for spontaneity or relaxation. It's always wise to allocate more time than you think you'll need. Don't forget, time is something you can never get back.

I can't stress enough about not losing sight of the very reason you decided to take your trip in the first place. Allow yourself to explore without a set timeframe to soak it all in, or switch off and put your feet up - after all, this is what holidays are about!

v) Add it all together

Add all the above together and you'll get the number of days you should dedicate to staying at the destination. Following this method is exactly why I ended up spending 9 days in Barcelona!

TIP: Avoid free days at museums and art galleries. Honestly, this is the time every man and his dog wants to go and you'll spend the majority of your day lining up to get in. I missed out on visiting the Picasso Museum in Barcelona as I had planned on visiting during the free day. The queue to get in was hundreds of metres in length; to me that wasted time could be better spent doing something else. In hindsight, I should have just sucked it up and planned to pay in full to support the museum on a regular day and not have to face a lengthy queue.

I always like to remind my readers, you can save money or time, usually not both. What is your time worth to you?

Selecting Accommodation

For some of us, deciding on where to stay when planning a trip can be a very overwhelming task. We are faced with so many questions when finding somewhere to rest our heads after a long day of sightseeing in a foreign land... What neighbourhood? Where to start?

After a decade of travelling and over 100 hotels later I'm here to help you turn this seemingly daunting task into a simple one. For me, location is king and I would much rather pay for the convenience of a nearby hotel than a luxury resort out of town requiring a commute to the city each day. Which would you prefer?

As I explain in each of my detailed itineraries on my blog, Invisible Tourists don't want to be wandering around a foreign city late at night in search of our next meal or knowing we have to trek for an hour to get back to our room. What a burden to have hanging over your head! This cuts into precious travel time where you could be enjoying yourself having a few drinks at a trendy new bar or devouring the local specialty dish at a family-run eatery.

But, if you stay too close to the action (depending on the city) you can expect a dreadful night's sleep from the sound of noisy streets or nightclubs outside your door. Is there a way to strike a balance?

How to choose the perfect hotel, every time

I've created a foolproof formula for finding the perfect hotel with a mid-range budget for each and every trip (by mid-range budget, I mean 3-4 star hotels and similar accommodation). Broken down into 5 simple steps for you, the formula isn't rocket science and hasn't failed me yet! Follow this step-by-step guide to find your ideal hotel and don't overthink it.

It's liberating to know you'll free up more time to enjoy all the awesome activities you'll be able to experience at your destination.

i) Investigate the neighbourhoods

If you don't know what neighbourhood you want to stay in, the first step for any destination is to find out where the heart of the city is. One way to do this is by using a guidebook or Google Maps as a reference. The first chapter of a guidebook and where Google Maps drops its little pin for your destination is usually the city centre, therefore the general vicinity of where to base your stay.

ii) Determine what is nearby

When zooming in on Google Maps (map view, not satellite), you'll notice the city will have areas of orange/yellow blocks lining the streets for your chosen neighbourhood. These are shops and eateries so it's a good idea to have some of these within a few moments' walk from your accommodation.

It's honestly worth paying a little extra to stay in these central locations. A hotel that's close to public transport such as train stations is invaluable when getting around (especially in larger cities such as London, New York or Tokyo). It's a bonus if the hotel is close to restaurants, convenience stores and other eateries. Even if this means the hotel is a street or two from a main road.

TIP: Where possible, try and select a hotel that is close to the attractions you wish to see. It's very handy to visit them only a short stroll from your hotel in the early mornings before tourist crowds arrive, or later in the evening once they are gone.

iii) Narrow down the options

I've used Booking.com throughout all my years of travel to search for hotels. Although I have been an affiliate since I began my blog, I have used their service for over a decade so it's easy for me to genuinely recommend them. Their map and filter options are all I need. With countless hotel options, there's too many to manually sift through so we need to narrow them down.

To do this, use the left sidebar to filter properties by review rating, budget and dates available. I usually opt for 8+ out of 10 from reviewers with a 3 or 4 star rating, depending on what you can get for your money in the city. Be sure to check recent photos to ensure the property is not overdue for a major renovation. This way there will be no nasty surprises on your arrival.

TIP: Don't forget to bring up the Google Street View of your chosen properties to check they aren't located on any sketchy-looking streets. Choose 3 properties where the location looks good and read the reviews.

iv) Read the reviews

While I personally use Booking.com to book my hotels as they offer the security of free cancellation and pay on checkout, I read reviews on TripAdvisor first. Booking.com tends to limit hotel reviews to favourable ones. We want the honest truth, which is easier to determine over on TripAdvisor.

Additionally, with over 800 million reviews, travellers tend to post more frequently on TripAdvisor. The reviewers may alert you to any construction or renovation works taking place at a property or nearby that may affect the quality of your stay. Sometimes traveller photos can set more realistic expectations than the professional hotel photos, too.

A great little perk of reading TripAdvisor reviews is the "Room Tips" feature. Here travellers reveal their secrets to securing the best rooms. This could be a unique view, feature, option for a room facing the rear of the property to avoid street noise, etc. Mention these in the "Special Requests" section at the time of your booking. For instance, I noted to request a corner room in my Hiroshima hotel and I managed to score a stunning 180° panoramic view over the entire city.

TIP: Don't forget to read any recent bad reviews. Sometimes people complain about niggly things that will have no impact on the outcome of your stay, such as hairline cracks in walls or a dent in the minibar door. That stuff isn't really a deal breaker. These reviews are still helpful because you can use your discretion and usually ignore them.

The honest experiences of other travellers who have stayed in a hotel before you are crucial to your decision-making process. The reviews of previous travellers have literally been my bible over the years. Once you've found a hotel that ticks all the boxes, book it in.

v) Book it in

Great location? Check. Option for a better room using "Room Tips" from TripAdvisor? Check. Within your budget? Check. Before getting out your credit card to make a payment, it's usually beneficial to cross-reference the prices with your chosen hotel directly.

Sometimes a property will provide incentives to book directly as popular booking platforms can take a percentage of the stay. I personally find Booking.com consistently has the best deals as their large market presence helps me receive the most bang-for-buck for a room. With the security of free cancellation in most cases, no hidden fees and option to pay at the property, I can always book with confidence.

Make your payment through the platform of your choice and just like that, you're done!

So there you have it, my 5 ridiculously simple steps for booking a perfect mid-range hotel every time. Now there's no excuse for staying in a dodgy neighbourhood that has a negative impact on your trip and tarnishes what could have otherwise been an incredible experience!

Case Study: Should You Use Unregulated Homestay Accommodation Services?

In recent years, the tourist vs traveller[56] debate began raging whereby a *tourist* was seen to have a negative connotation. Would-be visitors to a destination wanted to be known as a *traveller* who could visit a destination more "authentically" and "like a local." One way they hoped to achieve this was by avoiding regulated accommodation such as hotels and traditional B&B's in favour of residential properties available on homestay accommodation platforms.

The situation evolved into a monster in a very short timeframe, and as we examined earlier through the *Trends* section of Part II and *Negative Impacts of Tourism* section of Part III, UHA services promising cheap rentals for tourists became one of the multiple contributors to overtourism issues.

Fast forward to 2020, where the absence of tourism meant millions of these UHA listings sat empty across the globe. As hosts rushed to secure rents from local residents instead of tourists in Dublin, there was a rapid 64% increase[57] in short-term rentals returning to the long-term rental market.

As Invisible Tourists we want to support locals, not make their lives more difficult. Here are some reasons to reconsider using UHA in popular destinations you may not have thought of, but I also encourage you to not take my word for it and research these issues yourself for further reading.

i) Unregulated homestay accommodation services could be illegal in the city you're visiting

Just because there are listings for your destination doesn't mean the host and the UHA services are abiding by local laws. For instance, here are some facts that might make you think twice about using such services in the below major cities.

These are just a few examples and definitely not the only places where unregulated accommodation is problematic. I highly advise doing some research into your destination if you are considering using UHA platforms:

- In 2014, 72% of reservations made in New York City, USA were illegal.
- Almost half of holiday rentals in Barcelona, Spain are unlicensed according to the council.
- In 2015, 44% of advertised properties in Paris were permanently available for rental, despite laws stating holiday rentals are capped to only being available 120 days of the year.

- In 2018, Japan's crackdown on illegal homestay accommodation is said to have cost USD $10 million[58].

Another trend with UHA is illegal subletting. Statistics in Australia[59] revealed that 35% of listings are by people who don't even own the property, and without the knowledge of their landlord.

While tenants may not see an issue with secretly renting out their spare room on an UHA platform for extra cash, there are risks involved for both the tenant and property owner. The tenant could actually be in breach of their leasing agreement by having additional people reside in the property and distributing security keys without authorisation.

ii) Unregulated homestay accommodation can negatively impact locals' quality of life

While not unique to Palma de Mallorca, Spain, in 2018 short-term rentals sharply increased by 50% due to tourist demand, which resulted in residential rents rising by 40%. Housing became unaffordable for most local residents and pushed them out of their own city. Due to this, the island voted to ban UHA listings to make housing affordable for residents who needed to live and work.

Local residents in Kaisariani, Athens, claimed their neighbourhood actually became a "tourist hotbed" full of UHA rather than a residential area. The lack of tourism in 2020 meant their entire local area became a ghost town with short-term rentals usually reserved for tourists left sitting vacant.

iii) There's no housekeeping, reception or room service

Hotels employ dozens of locals to take care of things like housekeeping, reception, concierge services, kitchenhands and the like to keep the place running smoothly. To me, providing locals with jobs is quite important and staying in local-owned regulated accommodation supports this cause.

Additionally, the lack of a reception area with UHA means checking in and out with your host may not be flexible enough to suit your travel plans. And there is nowhere to leave your bags if you arrive before check-in or plan on leaving the city later in the day.

iv) You're at the mercy of your host

Even if a room is showing available, the host has the right to change their mind and cancel your booking at a moment's notice. Being left in limbo a few days before a trip and all other accommodation in the area being sold out is not an ideal situation to be in.

Let's not forget the potential issue of your host running late to meet you to exchange keys. This unaccounted-for delay could seriously affect your travel plans and may lead to you missing a crucial flight or train to your next destination. There isn't always time to wait around for someone to race from one side of the city to the other to collect keys!

With regulated accommodation (hotels, hostels, motels, traditional B&Bs, serviced apartments in areas zoned for tourists), times for checking in and out are made clear. During that period there is always someone there when you need to leave so it's simple to plan your journeys.

v) Do you really need an entire kitchen (and house)?

At the time of writing, statistics show 86% of UHA listings in Paris[60], France are whole apartments or houses. Booking an entire apartment or house for short-terms stays through UHA platforms results in fewer long-term rentals for local residents.

A lot of the time you don't really need an entire house or apartment with a kitchen when you're travelling short-term. Visiting a new place is all about getting out there and part of this is experiencing local, authentic food.

Dining out contributes to local economies by supporting jobs and businesses. Using your UHA to cook instant noodles in an effort to save money does not. Sorry, but it's true! Hotels and other regulated accommodation options provide basic amenities needed for your stay. If you really want a kitchen to cook for yourself due to allergies or other reasons, a serviced apartment (aparthotel) can fulfil this need.

vi) Privacy is never guaranteed

Perhaps your UHA host has also allowed friends to crash at their place during your stay and failed to mention it at any point. This may put a damper on the romantic weekend away you had planned with your partner as the intimate moments you were hoping for may not be so intimate after all!

Stories emerged about some UHA hosts using sneaky hidden cameras[61] in the bedrooms of their rentals on oddly-placed objects or random smoke alarms to monitor guests.

vii) Lack of safety and security regulations

Consistent standards and regulations are lacking across UHA rentals as they are basically private properties. Due to this hosts don't have to follow the same strict regulations that hotels do like fire, security and safety. What fire and other types of hazards are there in your rental? Can you tell from the photos?

Hosts who list on UHA also don't have to pay for the same insurances that hotels do, therefore if anything were to happen the UHA platform may not cover you at all. This also includes theft of your cash/valuables from the property, whether it was from the host, other guests or as a result of a break-in. Is there even a safe or secure place to store your valuables during your stay?

Additionally, some of the properties may not be very child friendly which is sometimes only possible to be discovered on arrival.

viii) Bait and switch

Bait and switch refers to the generally illegal act of "baiting" a guest into paying for a rental that is substituted for an inferior one later down the track. The intent is never to provide you the rental in the great location with amazing photos you paid for.

A host may contact you close to your arrival date to inform you of the change so you're made to think you're left with no other option but to accept the substandard accommodation they offer instead, sometimes even for more money!

This fraudulent trend is becoming more and more common with UHA. Sure it's also possible this can happen with smaller hotels as well, but is less likely as hotels have much more to lose by participating in this dirty practice. You can read more bait and switch stories[62] [63] to give you an idea of what could happen.

Case Study: In Summary

Ultimately, there is a time and a place for unregulated homestay accommodation. For instance, in rural areas where accommodation choices are slim, these platforms can actually help locals.

In major cities where there already is plenty of regulated accommodation, whole property rentals by hosts listing multiple properties should be avoided in order to help preserve local life and their culture.

By staying in a reputable, centrally located hotel, hostel, aparthotel or traditional B&B, you're helping to avoid contributing to issues affecting locals from UHA. These traditional accommodations are always in areas zoned for high pedestrian traffic and away from residential areas so they minimise disruption to locals.

There is certainly ample food for thought with this subject, don't you agree?

Ethical Alternatives to Unregulated Homestay Accommodation

Now we've examined all the issues with UHA services, it begs the question - are there any ethical alternatives? The answer is yes! There are sustainable services that can be used to help avoid contributing to overtourism issues. All it takes is a look back to the time before the sharing economy took off.

For transparency, with the exception of Booking.com I am not affiliated with any of the following companies and have not tried all these services personally. I am suggesting these alternatives as my travel philosophy aligns with each. Be sure to research further for yourself to determine which option is right for your circumstances.

While these options deliver on the promise of "living like a local," they won't inadvertently take long term rentals away from local residents:

- **Fairbnb.coop**
  Free for homeowners to list their properties, while 50% of the tourist's payment goes towards funding community projects chosen by locals at the destination. With the aim of promoting "authentic, fair and conscious tourism," hosts need to meet a set of criteria.

- **Traditional B&Bs (Bed and Breakfasts)**
  Security and privacy of a hotel, yet the property feels like home (because it *is* someone's home). Enjoy the provided breakfast and a chat with the host about their city, and gain insider knowledge about their favourite local establishments or fascinating sites not found in guide books. Regulated and in areas zoned for tourists.

- **Hotels, hostels and serviced apartments (aparthotels)**
  Adhere to consistent standards, local laws and are located in zones regulated for tourists or business travellers. This helps to minimise disruptions to local residents. A huge benefit is these options don't take any long-term accommodation off the market. Tourists are spread throughout a city in the appropriate areas rather than dominating residential neighbourhoods. Serviced apartments are also a great option for business travellers away from home who may need to stay for a longer period, and could benefit from a kitchenette.

- **Home exchange**
  Works by arranging reciprocal exchanges - where owners house swap on the same dates - or by using an accumulation of points to stay in another property whilst the owner is away. Staying in a completely residential area not overrun with vacation rentals allows travellers to better

blend in with locals, shop where they do, cook meals in the home and even get to know their temporary neighbours. Could be a great alternative for families who prefer multiple bedroom vacation rentals.

- **Housesitting**
  Housesitting allows you to temporarily stay rent free in return for taking care of the home whilst property owners are away. This could range from a few days to several months depending on the arrangement. Most of the time, responsibilities of housesitters include looking after pets, cleaning the home and basic garden maintenance.

- **Couchsurfing**
  Involves temporarily staying with a host for free in exchange for allowing others to also stay with you for free. It's not always necessarily on a couch, it may be in a spare bedroom or other common area within the home. Food isn't expected to be provided. As a guest you're able to share their bathroom and the host may be willing to show you around the neighbourhood. Couchsurfers have said they've made lifelong friends with their hosts/guests, making it a great way to meet people and a decent option for budget-conscious tourists.

How do we know if a B&B listing is ethical?

If using a service like Booking.com to find traditional B&Bs, how can we know if the listing is ethical or not?

It may be easier to determine in some locations than others, and may take a little extra research. The main differences between traditional B&Bs and residential properties in disguise is that traditional B&Bs are a form of hosted stays so the owner/employees should be present. These are the questions I'd ask to determine if a B&B is ethical or not:

i) Is the host going to be present during your stay?

When using the B&B filter on Booking.com, I'd avoid listings with "apartment" in the title. Some platforms mention whether you'll have the property all to yourself. The absence of a host and lack of reception/some kind of check in area would make me a bit skeptical as this could mean it's not an actual B&B but a residential property.

ii) Is breakfast provided?

Traditional B&Bs live up to their name - the host should be there to provide breakfast in the morning. This hospitality is what makes it a Bed & Breakfast, after all! Check if the property has its own website and the services they provide during your stay.

While breakfast may not be a requirement for all travellers, a traditional B&B will absolutely provide this service. If a full kitchen is provided and it's not a serviced apartment (aparthotel as mentioned earlier), chances are it's a residential property in disguise.

iii) Is the B&B listed on an official local tourism directory?

Check if the property is registered in a directory with the country's B&B association. In the times before smartphones, I remember hire cars in Ireland, the UK and New Zealand would come with an official B&B directory that listed regulated places to stay. It was easy to reference by each city, you could phone up to book throughout your trip or simply turn up to check they had vacancies. Examples of websites to use these days would be:

- Ireland - irishbnb.com
- New Zealand - bnb.co.nz

iv) What does the property look like at street level?

Check the Google street view. Traditional B&Bs usually have their name and "Vacancies/No Vacancies" signage out front, not just appear to be a residential property. However, if the owner is going to be present then you know the residential property will be a hosted stay at least.

v) Is the property listed on multiple platforms?

Google the B&B by name to cross-reference where else it's listed. What shows up? I'd also check if the host has more than one listing as that would be a red flag for me personally.

vi) Does the owner have a sustainable & ethical commitment to tourism?

If all the above fail, you could always reach out to the owner and ask their purpose for the listing. Do they only lease short term to tourists? Will they be present? Do they have other properties? How many days of the year do they rent their property to tourists? How long have they owned the property? Fairbnb has a set of strict guidelines their hosts need to adhere to, so these would be ideal for any ethical host to follow.

The common pattern shared by these suggested alternatives is that each ensures tourists can stay at a destination with confidence in knowing they aren't inadvertently taking residential properties away from locals. The even bigger win is a truly authentic local experience, not an artificial one.

Whether you're happy to sleep on a local's couch, prefer the privacy of a room or require fully-equipped homes, there is an ethical alternative to unregulated homestay accommodation services that aims to improve tourism for locals and tourists alike!

Opt for Direct Flights Instead of Multiple Cheap Ones

Booking a journey on a jet plane can be an exciting part of trip planning! Should you fly direct or look for flights with a few hours layover to save money? I'm aware flight comparison websites are very popular with would-be travellers, however I have never been a fan or used them. These websites usually omit direct flight options, instead only displaying cheap flights with multiple layovers.

Perhaps you can relate to this: Wanting to reach your destination as quickly as possible rather than spending hours unnecessarily waiting around in airport terminals! Even if that comes at a higher cost, personally I'm all for it to have the opportunity to spend more time exploring my destination. Time is a precious commodity. What is it worth to you?

From a responsible tourism standpoint, if you're undertaking more flights than necessary it can add up from an environmental perspective as take-off and landing uses the most fuel. If you want to take an extra step, you're able to offset carbon emissions for your flight.

TIP: As we examined in Part III, the cheapest options may not always be the most sustainable.

Reconsider Large Cruises & Day Trips to Popular Destinations

For selfish reasons, each day I looked forward to dusk in the medieval city of Bruges, Belgium. The sun setting over its stone bridges and old canals meant the unbearable crowds of day-tripping tourists had left the city for their accommodation elsewhere, leaving those of us remaining to breathe a sigh of relief.

The waterways bustling with tourist boats during the day became silent; overcrowded cobbled streets in the town's centre transitioned into unobstructed walkways illuminated by lamp post glow. Restaurants and eateries had tables available without the need to book, and dining al fresco without people bumping past chairs was an enjoyable treat.

Bruges after hours revealed a completely different, magical side to the city. I couldn't help but think of the thousands of tourists who skipped this opportunity to experience peacefulness that accentuates what makes Bruges unique.

To put things into perspective, did you know in 2019 out of Bruges' 8.6 million tourists, 6 million were day-trippers from cruise ships? On average they'd only spend 2-3 hours in the Belgian city. Not only does this mean they missed so much of what dear old Bruges has to offer, they also put enormous pressure on local infrastructure during a short timeframe.

Plan to stay longer at destinations popular with day-trippers

While sometimes compact destinations could be covered in one day, if they have been suffering from overtourism issues there's no need to avoid them altogether. The solution is to plan on staying at these destinations for several days.

How is staying longer an overtourism solution? It sounds counter intuitive, but hear me out.

Overcrowding at popular spots is all too easy as day-trippers rush around from place to place because their time is very limited. Travelling in this way can have a crushing impact on local's quality of life, and other tourists for that matter.

By staying longer at your destination, there's suddenly no need to cram everything into a short timeframe. You're able to visit popular tourist attractions during less busy periods, even visit some museums or galleries at night when the day-trippers and large tour groups are long gone. You'll be able to have a more enjoyable experience without the overwhelming burden of crowds and getting elbowed in the ribs every few moments!

Staying longer creates the opportunity to explore beyond the usual touristy sights into neighbouring suburbs. Discover the destination at a leisurely pace, stumble across a little-known café or museum not mentioned in guidebooks. Travelling in this way allows a more realistic view of the destination than you'd see superficially splashed about on social media or from a large (and rushed) group tour.

More time also means the freedom to engage with locals by booking in cultural experiences that take time. For instance, in Bruges this could be sampling locally-made beer on a brewery tour or enjoying a chocolate-making class. These hands-on experiences offer a greater appreciation and understanding of the local culture.

Booking experiences, Tickets, Organised Tours & Travel Essentials in Advance

As I approached Prinsengracht, one of Amsterdam's most well-known streets, I couldn't believe the queue made up of hundreds of tourists snaking down the canal-lined path and around the corner. They were waiting for an unknown length of time to visit Amsterdam's most beloved attraction, the Anne Frank Huis and museum.

I punctually walked to the front of the queue, confidently grasping a pre-purchased ticket in hand for my allocated time slot. A staff member scanned the barcode and I was let through in an instant. Looking over my shoulder briefly as I entered, I'll never forget the bewildered faces that gazed at me like I was some kind of magical unicorn!

If only those tourists were organised to have done the same as me and bought tickets 8 weeks in advance... It would have saved them endlessly waiting to see if there were any remaining tickets available for that day.

If you're anything like me, you absolutely HATE queues and prefer to spend time actually doing rather than waiting. Sometimes I think those who don't must enjoy lining up for tourist attractions. Are they the same people who camp out for days on end before the launch of the newest iPhone? Each to their own, but I just don't understand the appeal!

For many major attractions throughout the globe, it's possible to purchase some kind of advance ticket online to gain entry. In some cases, these advance purchases even allow you to skip the long queues to get in. The attraction may have their tickets listed through discounted online ticket vendors such as Klook (my personal favourite) or they may be sold exclusively through their own website.

As an example, Anne Frank Huis tickets can only be purchased exclusively through the foundation's website. To make the experience as respectful as possible, quotas are imposed on visitor numbers (perhaps the Château de Versailles should take note, right?).

For Anne Frank Huis, 80% of tickets for a given day can be purchased online up to two months in advance, while the remaining 20% are made available on-site to visitors on that day on a first-in-first-served basis. This means you could spend the better part of a day waiting to get in, only to find out that tickets have sold out as you approach the front of the queue. Don't make that mistake – plan ahead!

i) Booking Cultural Experiences

Having just finished a private tea ceremony with a *geiko* (Kyoto geisha) made possible with a local guide from MagicalTrip, I was chatting with him about my love of Japanese *sake* (alcoholic rice wine, pronounced *sa-keh*). He claimed, "You absolutely must try a rare red sake that can only be found in Kyoto while you're here. It doesn't get exported out of the region." Naturally, the exclusivity of this sake had me intrigued and with my busy last day ahead I doubted I'd have the chance to sample it before I left.

That evening I had a bar hopping tour scheduled with a different Kyoto guide. As he led our small group through the back alleys of the Pontocho area, I mentioned the red sake my morning guide had told me about. "Ah, I know just the place where you can try it!" he said, showing us the way to one of his favourite local bars.

As sake is usually clear or yellow tinged, I couldn't believe my eyes when the waiter brought a bright red glass over to my table. The vibrant colour was due to the sake being created from an ancient strain of red rice. Had it not been for these two local guides sharing their knowledge, I would not have had this serendipitous experience completely unique to Kyoto!

Participating in cultural experiences in a new country is one of the many reasons why I LOVE being a tourist. I can't stress this enough - take advantage of your glittering visitor status by booking meaningful experiences that help you learn more about local life, customs and culture from actual local residents.

Activities such as local walking tours, cooking classes, bar hopping nights, foodie tours and more that are unique to the destination can usually be booked a few days in advance on platforms such as Klook (or MagicalTrip for Japan specifically). Local guides can provide you with insights into the significance of things to their culture.

If your activity is not weather dependent, it will help to better plan your overall itinerary if you secure the date and time as soon as you can to avoid disappointment. That way you know you can organise the rest of your day around the experience.

TIP: Do a little research into the authenticity of the experiences if you can, and the companies you choose to book through. For instance, it wasn't until after I visited Barcelona that I learnt the popular flamenco shows actually aren't from the Catalan region of Spain and therefore not as authentic as they claimed to be - but actually staged authenticity for the sake of tourists.

ii) Booking Tickets

When visiting Milan, Italy I learnt a lesson the hard way, which is why I can't stress enough for you to research what's required for visiting attractions on your wishlist.

I was unsure whether I wanted to visit Da Vinci's famed *The Last Supper* fresco so I didn't bother booking a ticket in advance, rather waited to see how I felt once I was in Milan. During my 3 days in the city I decided I wanted to see it after all, and navigated the cobbled streets to Santa Maria delle Grazie where the mural is housed.

To my dismay I was informed that there was a four-day wait to get in without pre-purchased tickets (and this was during the off-season!).

Even if you would prefer to wait until the time closer to your arrival date before booking, it's always wise to check how soon in advance it's possible to buy tickets to popular attractions so you can make an informed decision. Do tickets sell out quickly, or are available a day or so in advance? Write yourself a note or set some kind of reminder to secure tickets as required, ensuring you don't miss out.

Take a look online for where to purchase tickets in advance for museums such as Musée du Louvre and Musée d'Orsay in Paris, art galleries such as the Museum of Modern Art in New York City, attractions such as the SkyTree in Tokyo and so on - Klook is a good place to start. Even attractions such as Claude Monet's Garden in Giverny, France allows advance ticket purchases through their own website.

TIP: Don't forget to check the cancellation policy for each in case your circumstances change. You may be offered a full refund or none at all.

For extremely popular attractions such as Musée du Louvre and Château de Versailles from Paris, you may wish to visit these outside of the usual hours for a more enjoyable experience without huge crowds. As an example, Château de Versailles has offered summer evening experiences where the magnificent gardens and fountains are beautifully illuminated at night to music.

iii) Booking Organised Group Tours

With dark wooden buildings lining its paved streets, thousands of decorated temples immersed in nature and centuries-old traditions held tightly to its chest, it's obvious to me why Kyoto is one of the most popular tourist destinations in Japan. The title of "World's Best City" from leading travel publication Travel + Leisure for two consecutive years (2014-2015) was very well deserved in my eyes.

Although, what may seem like a blessing can also become a curse.

To put things into perspective, both domestic and international visitors to Kyoto topped 53 million in 2019 - 40 million of whom were day-trippers[64]. Kyoto's local population is approximately 1.5 million people, which seems like a very small drop amongst a vast ocean of visitors.

I was saddened to see busloads upon busloads of day-tripping tourists on organised group tours during my 2019 visit; I don't recall seeing any during my 2014 stay in Kyoto. Numerous groups of 50 people poured out of coaches onto the narrow streets, creating a shuffling mosh-pit leading up to Kiyomizu-dera - Kyoto's beloved 1,300 year-old temple.

While their tour leaders waved little pointy flags along the iconic Sannenzaka street, these crowds were noisy, pushy and completely ruined the ambience of what felt like a calm and peaceful ancient capital only a few years prior. Tourists were too busy trying to shuffle past one another that no one was venturing into the local businesses lined along the street.
In a car park just off Sannenzaka, I noticed twelve coaches parked. There were enough parking spaces in that lot for 42 coaches, so if we make some calculations:

- 42 coaches x 50 people in each = 2,100 day-trippers crammed into this relatively compact area of Kyoto at any given time
- Not including the spaces for regular cars with their passengers.

These centuries-old streets were definitely feeling the strain, not necessarily designed for such numbers.

Whether it's for a short day venture or several weeks, organised tours can be a great way to squeeze more out of your travel time. If there's anything I've learnt in recent years however, not all organised tours are created equal. What was happening in Kyoto during 2019 unfortunately wasn't exclusive to this city, with similar stories emerging from numerous destinations globally.

What to look for when selecting organised group tours

While I strive to encourage independent travel on my blog,

there's no denying there are benefits of using organised tours at times. When selecting an organised tour, it's important to weigh up the benefits versus potential negative impacts of small and large groups - regardless of whether they are tours for a few hours, a day or multiple-destination group tours that span several days or weeks.

To define group numbers, small tours should be no more than 12-14 participants, while large tours can be up to 50 people. The positive and negatives of small and large group tours include:

Positives of large group tours

- Prices are low and competitive due to large numbers
- Able to visit many locations in an efficient manner
- Meet other tourists
- Relax as all the planning has been done for you
- No need to worry about navigating the local public transport as the tour uses a private coach.

Negatives of large group tours

- Large groups can be intimidating for locals and fellow tourists (with little accountability for those misbehaving)
- Rush around the the main sights during peak times, with a brief introduction to each
- Large tourist numbers make the experience impersonal
- Provided with information rather than feeling rewarded by finding it out on your own
- Exclusively using private transport could mean not experiencing the local way of life.

Positives of small group tours

- Smaller groups can blend in amongst locals more easily
- Able to visit a few locations in an efficient manner, sometimes outside of peak times

- Meet other tourists, or be completely private for couples if preferred
- Relax as all the planning has been done for you
- No need to worry about navigating the local public transport as your guide may use it with you
- Walking or cycling tours are better for the environment
- A more personalised, authentic experience where the pace can be controlled by you
- Don't need to wait around for anyone
- More individual time with the tour guide to ask questions.

Negatives of small group tours

- Prices are more expensive due to small numbers
- I honestly can't think of any others!

As you can see, there are some points that overlap in both small and large group tours. To take a sustainable approach, Invisible Tourists would almost always opt for the smaller tour. Sure, this means you may need to add extra into your budget for these kinds of experiences but I promise you'll get so much more out of them!

The only exception to selecting a large group tour would come into play if it's planning on going to destinations that have ample space for visitors and the local population is not at risk from overtourism problems. For instance, I didn't mind taking a bus tour around Lake Kawaguchi near Mt Fuji in Japan because this destination has ample space for tourists to spread out around the region.

Tips for booking organised tours

- For multiple-destination organised tours, book as soon as you can to ensure a place on your preferred date of departure. This may be several months or even a year in advance, but if it's more of a last-minute decision, call the

tour company to see if they have room to squeeze you in.
- For organised day tours at your destination try to book in advance where possible, maybe around a week or so once you know the weather forecast for your desired day. As weather conditions are one of the few things outside of our control, I always suggest staying several days at your destination to offer some flexibility. If you can book online with instant confirmation, it's even better.
- In order to not contribute to overtourism issues at popular locations from day-trippers, look for day tours that limit the capacity of tourists to no more than 12-14 people.

Wherever you're planning to visit, look for tour companies whom:

- Select locally-owned accommodation where possible
- Employ local residents
- Have a clear animal welfare policy
- Work to ensure every link in their supply chain is ethical
- Comply with the Modern Slavery Act of 2015 to ensure no aspect of their business is engaged with modern slavery or human trafficking.

For Asia, companies such as InsideJapan Tours and its parent InsideAsia Tours have a strong focus on travelling in a sustainable way. I have personally toured with InsideJapan once myself, and to be transparent I paid for my tour in full with my own money and am not affiliated with them in any way. I was so impressed with the ethos of InsideJapan. Our philosophies towards travel closely align, so it is easy for me to genuinely recommend their small organised group tours to my readers who prefer not to go it alone.

Carefully observing their responsible approach to tourism during my trip, I can attest to InsideJapan's commitment to ensuring our tourist footprints were as minimal as possible. We visited offbeat destinations and alternatives to popular spots, stayed at local family-run accommodation, and our small group size was personable. We were immersed in cultural experiences and had the ideal amount of free time to explore at our own pace.

In my eyes InsideJapan has truly set a high benchmark for organised tour groups. My experience was such a refreshing contrast to my very first package tour of Europe, and I cannot stress enough how much more fulfilling the experience was overall!

If you plan to book an organised tour, I strongly recommend looking at similar companies in different regions across the world who offer these kinds of small group experiences.

Travel Essentials You May Have Forgotten About

What travel essentials will you need for your trip? It's possible to book things like portable wifi, SIM cards, train tickets and other transport passes before you even step foot in your destination. This is an especially good idea for countries like Japan where there can be a language barrier and having access to phone data for Google Maps helps to navigate around with ease.

The online booking platform Klook, mentioned earlier and with whom I am a proud affiliate partner, connects local vendors with visitors to help plan a stress-free trip. Not only is Klook perfect for booking travel experiences but also to reserve essential transport passes and technology in advance. And no, they didn't pay me to sing their praise - I can genuinely recommend the platform as I use it myself!

Some transport passes and exchange vouchers can be mailed to your home before embarking on your journey, while other bookings may have an express queue for online ticket holders once you arrive at the destination. If you're not familiar with Klook, my detailed guide[65] covers everything you need to know to better organise your future trips.

Some other travel essentials you may have forgotten about include:

- **Packing cubes:** Seriously, these are a game changer and great for keeping your belongings organised when temporarily living out of a suitcase.
- **Universal travel adaptors:** Having one or two of these saves you from carrying around multiple other kinds for different countries.
- **Travel wallet:** Used for keeping passports, boarding passes, transport tickets and other important documentation all in one place for easy reference.
- **Eye mask for sleeping:** Sometimes you can't be sure of how much light window shades will block out at your upcoming accommodation. Having an eye mask handy is ideal for folks like me who need their room to be very dark in order to sleep.
- **Travel card holder:** Leave your regular wallet or purse at home with all those loyalty cards and items you won't need abroad. A small travel card holder just needs to fit your credit card and enough cash to get through the day (as your keycard and remaining cash should be left in your hotel safe).
- **Smartphone apps:** I'm not someone who is huge on using apps for things in day-to-day life, however for travel I have a small handful of essential apps that I can recommend:

  - **TripIt** is amazing for organising your itinerary, especially for long-term travel where you have multiple months' worth of accommodation and flights to collate. It's also great for creating a final PDF of the entire itinerary to send to family or friends. I've used TripIt since 2012 and highly recommend the free version.
  - **XE Currency** to keep track of fluctuating exchange rates whilst you're away.
  - **Klook** for booking cultural experiences on the go if you have extra time.

- **TripAdvisor** for the sole purpose of reading reviews about accommodation.
- **Google My Maps** to download an offline version of the destination for when you don't have access to wifi. If you create a map in advance, you'll be able to drop pins at locations of interest to reference later.

Why You Shouldn't Always Buy the Tourist Pass

Know what types of tourist or transport passes are available for your destination and don't always blindly buy them assuming they offer good value. Oftentimes these passes have limitations or allow discounted entry into several attractions that you may not even want to visit.

Weigh up the cost of the pass versus if you were to only pay for experiences you want. You may be surprised!

If you're familiar with my Japan travel itineraries, you'll know I've experienced travelling around the country on several occasions with and without the popular Japan Rail Pass (JR Pass). While the pass does provide great value for money if you plan to undertake three *shinkansen* (bullet train) journeys, its limitations meant I didn't bother with the pass for my first trip.

As an example, the JR Pass doesn't cover the fastest bullet trains, *Nozomi* and *Mizuho*. By paying for the exact services I wanted rather than waiting for slower trains, I was able to save over five hours of travel time during a two week trip. This meant I was able to maximise time at my desired destinations.

TIP: I've noticed when some people buy the rail pass they feel obligated to use it at any opportunity so travel becomes the focus of the trip, rather than the destinations themselves. Try and avoid this if you can, as this could be applied to transport passes in any country.

Here's another example. While we're on the subject of the JR Pass in Japan, it's annoying to use for a day trip from Hiroshima to Miyajima, a popular sacred island nearby. A direct 45 minute ferry ride to Miyajima is possible from Hiroshima's centrally located Peace Memorial Park. The direct ferry is not covered by the JR Pass.

If you wish to use the JR Pass for your journey to the island, it involves a tram, train and ferry ride taking 1.5 hours each way. At 3 hours of travel time, this inefficient option takes double the time needed for the direct ferry. I'd much prefer to spend that extra time exploring the island itself than being in transit. In these instances try to remember: what is your time worth to you?

Consider Ethics Around Animals in Tourism to be a Responsible Tourist

Thankfully it hasn't been all doom and gloom for the tourism industry in recent years. Some positive shifts have happened, too.

On my first visit to Santorini, like thousands of other tourists I rode a donkey up the almost 600 stairs from the port to Old Town. At the time, this was the "done thing" to do without much thought, just like riding an elephant in Thailand or petting an owl in an animal café in Japan.
Long story short, I was placed on a juvenile donkey that was obviously so exhausted from doing this day in, day out that he tripped and fell, causing me to tumble off onto the concrete steps.

This was a huge wake-up call to me about animal welfare in tourism and I felt awful that the donkey was obviously suffering, so I climbed the remaining stairs myself. A few years later, I revisited Santorini and did the donkeys a favour by catching the cable car up to the Old Town from the port instead. The views were just as great and it didn't take anywhere near as long to reach the top!

According to World Animal Protection[66], over half a million wild animals are used in tourism. It pains me to say I was guilty of contributing to this trend back in the day. Luckily for me, all I needed was one time to hit my head on concrete during my earlier travels to make me realise I didn't want to be a part of this ever again.

I'm really pleased to see that today, over ten years on, more attention is being brought to animals who suffer to gather tourist money and what alternatives there are instead. Ethical animal sanctuaries[67] are popping up in Asia, North America and Africa.

As discussed earlier in Part II, this rise in awareness and change of attitudes towards unethical animal tourism[68] has seen tourists reconsider the following experiences and I kindly urge you to do so, too:

-
- Paying for selfies with any chained animals
- Riding animals for short periods such as camels, elephants and donkeys
- Visiting exotic animal cafés and villages in Japan
- Visiting travelling circuses that feature wild animals
- Visiting zoos where wild animals are kept in dreadful living conditions
- Visiting aquariums where dolphins and whales are kept in captivity.

I think it's great that people have become more vocal about the mistreated animals in tourism that don't have a voice. Although as tourists we may have made mistakes in the past (myself included), it's important we learn from them and not repeat them moving forward. This is using our hidden power to create effective change that is so desperately needed!

Overview: Before a Trip

When laying foundations for our future trips, we can take advantage of strategies to help us avoid looking like tourists once we're at our destination by ensuring we are:

- Doing our best to travel during the least busy times where possible to avoid contributing to overcrowding.
- Staying in central (and regulated) accommodation to allow us to visit popular places before day trippers arrive and after they leave. It also means won't inadvertently take rental properties from local residents.
- Creating a wishlist of attractions beforehand and including time to relax to help us determine the length of our upcoming stay.
- Selecting direct flights where possible as this is both time and energy efficient.
- Booking tickets to popular attractions and cultural experiences in advance to prevent having to queue up unnecessarily, or be disappointed by missing out on things we looked forward to.
- Avoiding unethical animal encounters to drive positive change in the industry.
- Forgoing large cruises to minimise economic leakage and benefit from staying longer at popular destinations. This means exploring beyond popular sights, skipping crowds and having a more enjoyable, relaxed experience.

DURING A TRIP

Being Invisible: How to Not Look Like a Tourist

Now we've reached the part that outlines the juicy details you can implement to combat the challenges and problems we examined in the first half of this book. I'm sure by this stage you're wondering how it's even possible to be *invisible* during a trip, especially if your ethnicity is different to your host country's. Is it *really* that big a deal if you look like a tourist?

Take this story for instance. I met a girl on a flight to New York who was robbed of her iPhone and wallet within her first 30 minutes of arriving in Paris. This astonished me as I'd visited France's capital four times and never had an issue.

While I listened to her story in absolute surprise at first, I soon realised she practiced all the hallmarks of a stereotypical tourist. Her actions gave her away to thieves at Gard du Nord station gates - she had headphones in, iPhone out on display, wallet in her back pocket. Oblivious to her surroundings, the valuables were ripe for the picking.

These kinds of situations are avoidable if you don't appear to be a distracted tourist.

On a more positive note, blending in has LOADS of benefits. From meeting locals to avoiding pesky pickpockets and scammers, it really is the best way to get the most out of your travel experience!

I'm not sure why many other travellers are not aware of these steps (or don't care about them) but it's really simple to avoid looking like a tourist when you're exploring somewhere new. It doesn't even take much effort.

Think about locals and expats. Expats are at almost every destination around the world and they get out and about, don't they? So what defines you as a tourist, expat or local isn't necessarily just about the way you look. How you act and your behaviour is what will give you away!

Here's what you can do to avoid looking like a tourist during a trip - irrespective of your heritage - at any destination.

Know the Importance of Dressing Appropriately

This may seem obvious but it's one of the most important steps. If you truly want to blend into a crowd, don't wear anything that will draw attention to you such as that colourful Hawaiian shirt or baseball memorabilia from home.

Additionally, it's imperative to be respectful of local cultures and customs. In some temples throughout Asia and the Middle East, shoes must be removed before entering - take a cue from what the locals are doing. In many religious sites throughout the world, women need to cover their hair, shoulders and even knees.

TIP: Ladies, it's always a good idea to throw a light scarf or shawl into your suitcase to use for multiple purposes.

Also included in what not to wear when abroad is active wear. Yes, this is an unpopular opinion! If you're visiting museums, art galleries and places of worship active wear really isn't appropriate for the occasion. It also screams *tourist!* Leave the active wear at home for when you're working out, please and thank you.

In general, what to wear to not look like a tourist

Branded designer clothing and handbags scream "Look at me, I'm not from here" in a majority of destinations. While this may be acceptable and a bit of a status symbol at home, in many countries it can come across as pretentious and can make you an obvious target to pickpockets.

It helps if you do a little research into the destination you're visiting beforehand, too. For instance, locals in cities like Tokyo and Paris dress smartly, or smart casual. Whereas in other destinations such as Dublin or Los Angeles it's more acceptable to dress down and wear sneakers on a night out.

What to wear to not look like a tourist in Europe

I see this question asked quite a lot so I'm going to make a generalisation here. The honest truth is smart casual works for most European destinations - no training shoes, backpacks, ripped jeans, baseball caps or active wear. Europeans are usually stylish, wear colour blocked clothing in cities rather than bright patterns, and prefer structured handbags rather than slouchy.

Ladies, a small yet stylish crossbody bag will go a long way to differentiating yourself from the average tourist. Nothing flashy with designer labels screaming for attention, just a simple, understated bag will do.

Remember if you're in a place where the average local would not wear flashy things then you probably shouldn't either. For example, I know of travellers who had their designer coats and other items stolen from cloak rooms[69] in Prague nightclubs. Moral of the story: Don't travel with something you couldn't bear to part with, either!

Be Culturally Aware by Practicing the Local Customs & Etiquette

While walking around eating may seem completely acceptable at home, did you know this is frowned upon in Japan? Or that you should never touch a child on their head in Thailand? Or why ladies should never place their handbag on the floor in China? Or why you shouldn't smile at strangers in Russia?

It's crucial to learn local customs and etiquette before your trip - and put them into practice during your trip - in order to not look like a clueless tourist. Not only will this demonstrate to locals that you respect their cultural heritage, they'll be appreciative of your efforts!

Some basic destination-specific customs and manners you should research before your trip are:

- **Knowing how to greet people:** Do you shake hands, kiss on the cheek (and how many times) in Europe, or bow in Asia?
- **How to behave on public transport:** Is speaking on the phone frowned upon? Should you form an orderly queue to get on or off the train? Or is it more of a free-for-all?
- **Mannerisms:** Is showing the sole of your shoe whilst sitting going to cause insult in some parts of Asia or the Middle East? Are you supposed to take your shoes off when entering places of worship? Should you use your left hand when handling merchandise or shaking hands in India, Sri Lanka, the Middle East and parts of Africa?
- **Punctuality:** Is it considered rude to keep people waiting at a meeting or group gathering, or acceptable to be fashionably late?
- **Tipping:** Is it considered necessary as it is in the United States, or an insult as it is in Japan and South Korea?
- **Gifting:** What should you bring if invited to a local's home? Why should yellow flowers be avoided in Russia, and an uneven number preferred? Should you avoid giving sharp

objects as gifts in the Netherlands? Why should gifts in sets of four be avoided in China and Japan?

- **Dining out:** Should you clean your plate completely, or leave a small portion of your meal behind to signify you were given enough food in parts of Asia and Russia? Do you call on the waiter/waitress or wait for them to approach you? Should you loudly slurp your noodles as a sign of appreciation to the chef in Japan? Is it considered an insult to ask for salt in Egypt? Is it acceptable to eat with your bare hands, cutlery or chopsticks?
- **Crossing the road:** Do you wait for the green signal in Germany or Japan, or is it socially acceptable to cross the road at any time? In Italy or Vietnam, will the traffic stop for you if you jump out in front of it?
- **Toilets:** Will they be porcelain bowls like Western Europe and the United States, or traditional squatting toilets throughout Asia?

These are just a few things you should keep in mind and put into practice during your trip to avoid looking like a tourist.

Optional: Learn some local expressions

Every country has their own quirky sayings and expressions. In Australia, "she'll be right, mate" means everything is going to be okay, and "what's the craic?" in Ireland is another way to say "what's happening." If you know these kinds of little sayings, locals are going to absolutely love you!

When encountering locals in my travels, I always let them know about Australia's "drop bears." If you haven't heard of these mythical beasts, they're koalas bearing sharp teeth that specifically drop out of trees onto unsuspecting tourists. The only way to soothe them is by offering them Vegemite. Quirky local tales such as these make the perfect conversation starters.

With the help of fellow guest bloggers from around the globe, The Invisible Tourist covers customs and correct etiquette in dozens of destinations across several continents. Take a look at my "Be Invisible" series[70] to help get you started and prevent making a social faux pas.

Become Familiar With Some Language Basics

I'll give you a little backstory as to why I'm so passionate about learning languages for travel. My first visit to France many moons ago, I was linguistically unprepared. I'd barely learnt French beforehand but had learnt a little Spanish. And it showed. I kept getting the words confused (because Spanish and French share many similar words) and it resulted in a hostile reception from many locals I encountered... Oops!

You can see why the French have a reputation for being rude... Wait. Was it them, or was it something I was doing? I can tell you it was *definitely* all me. It was a completely negative experience and it drew attention to the fact I was a tourist. I may as well have had a flashing neon sign on my forehead. So when I revisited France a year later, I was determined to learn as much French as possible so I could be an Invisible Tourist this time. And you wouldn't believe what happened.

I emerged from my clueless tourist cocoon and became *invisible*, owing this transition to one of the most memorable nights of my life in Paris with a group of locals. My travel buddy and I got chatting with some Parisians in a sports bar, the night kicked on and before I knew it, we were welcomed to a "lock in" - the bar was closed to the public and the few of us remaining inside were treated to free, unlimited drinks until the early hours. My sides were aching from the laughter!

Did I care that I had a 6am flight the next morning? A little, but there was no way I was going to pass up that crazy opportunity to have an amazing time with locals. That night I learnt there is no word for "hangover" in French, "snail's head" is the correct term!

Learning some language basics of your destination is probably one of the most crucial tips and will earn you massive brownie points with locals - you've gone to the effort to learn their native tongue and demonstrate that you respect them and their cultural heritage. It's like waving a golden ticket at a local and a big confidence boost for you to do things you may not have considered otherwise.

Not convinced yet? Learning what you need is easier than you think.

Benefits of learning language for travel

You could always whip out your smartphone with Google Translate whilst on the go, but that's bound to get annoying. In my case, it can even feel a little like cheating at times unless I'm really stuck!

I've learnt some of these the hard way so you don't have to. There are many advantages of learning a language for travel purposes, but in a nutshell these are:

- **Won't look like a lost tourist:** If you can read even the basic signage in a foreign language you won't need to ask for as many directions when you're getting around. Looking like you know where you're going means you won't draw unwanted attention to yourself, and you'll be able to get to your destination more efficiently.
- **Dining out:** It's super handy for knowing what to order when you're perusing a menu and inspecting the bill (cheque/check for my American readers) at the conclusion

of your meal. If you have allergies or follow a particular diet, you'll also know what foods to avoid.

- **Reading the alphabet:** When English menus aren't available, it can be helpful just to read the alphabet of your target language. For instance when I was in Athens, I couldn't completely read a menu in Greek but by sounding out the words, I could make out what some were. Turns out *καλαμάρι* aloud spells calamari!

- **Similar languages:** If you learn one language, it may be helpful with another similar one you haven't fully learnt. For instance, when I went to a dry cleaner in Madrid I had forgotten the Spanish word for "cold" *(frío)* but remembered the French word for it *(froid)*. The lady quickly understood what I wanted, which was a cold wash only.

- **Won't sound like a clueless tourist:** Taxi drivers are less likely to rip you off if you greet them in their native tongue (this includes knowing which of Switzerland's four languages to use in each region so as not to annoy the driver... I know this from personal experience, haha).

- **Positive reception:** You'll get a much warmer reception from locals if you can greet, farewell and speak a few basic phrases of their language. I can't stress this enough!

- **Personable experiences:** Finally, you'll feel all warm and fuzzy knowing you warmed someone else's heart purely because you spoke their language. You'll earn the highest level of respect from locals, which results in positive travel experiences.

How to learn language for travel purposes

With a variety of different resources available, it's never been easier to begin learning a language for travel by teaching yourself. The best news is you don't have to be totally fluent. On the contrary, far from it (thank goodness, right?).

No need to stress about learning it all. The trick is to learn enough of the language so you can ask for help if you need it and tell locals a little about yourself whilst on your adventure. I strongly recommend learning a few essential phrases (and possible responses) of your target language as a bare minimum to get you by. This has worked wonders for me!

Essential phrases to learn

I promise learning language for travel purposes doesn't have to seem so daunting. Truthfully, you don't need to spend years becoming fluent. Just learn the words and phrases you'll need - forget learning the rest if you prefer. Your main focus should be:

- **Greetings:** Saying hello, introducing yourself and what country you're from
- **Niceties:** Words for please, thank you, good morning, good evening, you're welcome
- **Farewells:** Saying goodbye, see you soon
- **Dining out:** Ordering food, drinks, asking for the bill (cheque/check), words to politely ask "what is this/that?"
- **Retail:** Clothes sizing, buying items with credit cards
- **Asking where to find something:** Toilets, points of interest, train platforms, restaurants
- **Numbers:** Helpful for shoe or clothing sizes, ordering quantities of something, etc
- **What to say in an emergency:** Help, stop, thief, etc.

Yes, that's pretty much it. Hopefully, you'll never need to use the last one but it's useful to have up your sleeve!

Top resources to help you learn a language for travel

Get your hands (and ears) onto some audio resources. Listening to the audio in the car, around the house or on the train during my daily commute to work helped me hear the correct pronunciation and speak with the correct accents.

You can read as much as you like to try and get the correct pronunciation, however nothing really beats hearing the words by a native speaker to help you learn. Listening will give you the confidence to know you're pronouncing words correctly once you arrive at your destination.

These days there are countless apps to assist with your foreign language learning, but it can seem like wading through mountains of them to find suitable candidates. What works for one person may not work for the next as we all learn differently.

Thankfully there are more ways to learn than just mobile apps. Some resources to help you learn your target language for travel purposes include:

- Lonely Planet, Berlitz phrasebooks or textbooks (with audio)
- Language for travellers courses at your local university or community college
- Free apps such as Memrise and Duolingo
- YouTube videos by native speakers or those who are fluent in your target language
- Pinterest for infographics and cheat sheets of your target language.

After a little experimenting, you'll find the resources that work best for you.

TIP: Want to up your language game ever further? Aspire to get beyond transactional interactions with locals to forge meaningful conversations by finding common interests. This is how my travel buddy and I found ourselves locked into that Parisian bar I spoke about earlier! We kept in touch with our new French friends and caught up with them once they travelled from Paris to Sydney.

It's usually best to avoid politics, controversial subjects and sensitive topics in order to not cause unintended offence. Some examples of conversation starters are:

- This is my first trip here, what would you recommend I shouldn't miss?
- Tomorrow is my last day here, it has been...
- I think my ancestors are from this area...
- Have you ever been to...
- What do you enjoy doing in your spare time?

Explore With a Healthy Dose of Skepticism

Travelling with a healthy dose of skepticism can mean the difference between falling for a scam or not. In order to survive a summer in Europe (or most destinations really) without being scammed you need to think almost EVERYONE who approaches you is out to get you... Seriously. I know, I know, this sounds totally harsh and even a little bit scary, but it truly works and helps you prevent putting yourself in an avoidable situation.

If someone is displaying unwanted interest in you, it is usually some sort of scam. It's a sad reality as I understand some people are just trying to make a living, but if you stop and buy something from one person, you attract many more or fall victim to their deceit.

How often are you responsive to relentless telemarketers at home? This is the abroad off-phone equivalent. If you want something yourself you usually go and get it on your own, not from a random stranger on the street with a hidden agenda.

TIP: Speaking from first-hand experience, one exception to this rule is Japan. People tend to keep to themselves and won't approach you - unless you've genuinely dropped something and they wish to give it back! It's such a refreshing change from other destinations.

Know the sneaky scams at your destination

Some tourist hotspots around the world are notorious for scamming visitors, particularly Paris, Barcelona, Prague and south-east Asian countries just to name a few. Fortunately for me, I've visited many major cities across four continents and can proudly say I've never fallen victim to a scam or been robbed (touch wood!).

But how? In notorious areas I never let my guard down. Being curious, prepared and observant of my surroundings helps to eliminate risks and recognise suspicious behaviour.

It's easy to check if there are any scams at your destination by doing a quick search online to prepare yourself in advance and avoid taking the bait. The rough guide to 40 tourist scams[71] can give you an idea of what to expect at various locations.

Fake It 'til You Make It to Avoid Looking Like a Tourist

Always look like you know where you're going, even when you don't. Locals always know where they're going, so to blend in with them you need to act the part. If you really are lost, forget consulting a map in a busy area or wandering aimlessly with your phone out. Your cover will be blown, pickpockets will catch on and you may become an easy target in crowded areas.

Instead, consult your map or phone inside a store or café before moving on. You can also approach a local who seems like they have somewhere to be (not a person who is loitering around a tourist hotspot, they can be trouble). Politely ask them in the local language if they have a moment to give you directions.

Locals appreciate you making the effort to learn their language and will be happy to help. Don't be afraid, you've got this.

TIP: Avoid travelling as part of a large group where possible. It's obvious when a huge gathering of people are following someone with a little flag that it's a group of tourists who haven't a clue where they're going!

Use Public Transport Where You Can

Private transfers from airports to hotels are usually expensive. If you'd truly like to experience the local way of life at your destination, catch the train, bus or taxi. Not only do you get the full experience but you are supporting local jobs and keeping these services running. An added bonus in some cases it can be a cheap way to get around!

There are some exceptions to this, however.

- **Time of day:** Aim to use these services outside of commuting hours wherever possible. In some of the busiest train networks in the world such as Tokyo, London and New York City, there just may not be room for you and your suitcase on crammed commuter trains. Trying to squeeze on a packed train is a stress you may be able to avoid with forward planning.
- **Don't abuse public transport systems:** For instance Tram 28 in Lisbon, Portugal has become so overcrowded with tourists wanting to get around the city on the cheap that locals often need to wait an hour to catch them to work. As tourists, we should have more time to relax and enjoy our travels so walking on foot is a great alternative, or use these services outside commuting hours as to not inconvenience locals during peak times.
- **Use taxis with caution:** If planning to use taxis at your destination, do some research online in travel forums about the likelihood of tourists getting ripped off in some cities. In the instance where taxi drivers are known to charge tourists a small fortune, it may be wise to book an airport transfer through your hotel or arrange privately through a platform like Klook.

On heading from our hotel to the airport in Madrid, Spain our taxi driver drove completely out of the way in order to rack up a substantial fare. I felt as though we were driving around in circles until my partner confirmed we actually were. That annoying pang hit me in the pit of my stomach knowing we were about to be ripped off.

We didn't want to cause a scene (as sometimes this can wind up in a worse situation if authorities get involved) so paid the ridiculous fare and went inside the airport for our flight. We realised taxis were so plentiful in Madrid's airport that even locals didn't use them (no wonder!). To contrast this in Barcelona, a high turnover of locals were also using taxis in addition to tourists so it seemed we were less likely to be ripped off. Thankfully we weren't.

TIP: Look up what the average taxi fare should cost heading to or from an airport before your journey so you're aware. Confirm it with the driver beforehand for extra peace of mind and to avoid an expensive lesson. Some cities such as New York have a flat fee of USD 52 from JFK airport to downtown Manhattan. Another idea is to negotiate a fixed fare with the driver before hopping in the taxi.

Also, take note of the official taxi pick up areas to avoid any illegal drivers operating at your destination. In cities such as Paris, "friendly" but unlicensed taxi drivers may approach tourists at major airports or train stations in order to extort money from them. For instance, a Thai couple were charged €247 by an unlicensed driver[72] from Charles de Gaulle airport to central Paris, a journey that should have only cost €55 under the city's flat rate scheme.

Avoid Permanently Displaying Your Camera & Selfie Stick

To some tourists, cameras are a status symbol. The bigger the lens, the better, right? Well, the number of tourists I've seen over the years with these hugely expensive SLR cameras and leaving its flash on when they're shooting an object behind a glass cabinet or window... *Facepalm.*

Unless you're a professional photographer, do you really need a flashy camera permanently draped around your neck that makes you look like a tourist? If you don't know how to use it correctly, expensive gear just doesn't seem worth the effort.

How to not look like a tourist with a camera

A compact and discreet camera that easily fits in a small bag will do the trick. It's wise to invest in a good mirrorless like my Canon G7X Mark III. It's a great compromise from a big SLR and even shoots video in 4k!

Additionally, nothing bellows "tourist" louder than someone that documents their every move on their phone with a selfie-stick (urghhh). I know I'll be in the minority with this opinion BUT I cannot stand selfie sticks. They're invasive, annoying, and have caused so many issues that many cities across the globe have banned them in public areas, museums and the like.

Don't Flash That Cash

Do your best to refrain from displaying massive wads of cash. Better yet, don't carry much cash at all, if you can help it. Many places accept credit or debit cards so these days the need for carrying cash isn't really there in many destinations.

It's important to note tourists of Asian heritage are especially vulnerable in Europe because pickpockets know they usually carry large sums of cash when they travel to purchase luxury goods[73]. I'm sorry to say it's unfortunate but true!

TIP: If you do need to carry cash in some smaller towns, take enough with you for that day and leave the rest in your hotel safe.

Be Mindful When Dining Out

Support small local businesses and their families by hunting around for where the locals go to eat. It's a win-win situation because not only is this where you'll find the tastiest, most authentic food of your destination, you're also less likely to get ripped off by tourist trap restaurants that have swarms of one-off visitors going through eating their mediocre food.

If you happen to chat to any locals when you're out and about, ask them where they would recommend you go. Even staff at your hotel or traditional B&B should be able to provide you with a local's perspective.

Enjoying the local cuisine where locals do helps support small businesses and minimise economic leakage. As mentioned earlier, you'll be able to do more of this with your hotel in close proximity so you can spend more time out enjoying yourself.

Reduce, Reuse, Recycle

While these could be considered traits of a sustainable tourist, sustainability falls under responsible tourist behaviour. As individuals these choices may seem like a drop in the ocean overall, however as we know small actions multiplied over hundreds (if not thousands) of people can quickly add up!

Here are a few ways you can reduce, reuse and recycle when travelling to minimise negative impacts on the environment and infrastructure of a destination:

- **Reduce** your shower time at your accommodation to help preserve local water supplies.

- **Reuse** your hotel linens such as towels and sheets during your stay. This helps reduce the amount of unnecessary industrial washing.
- **Reuse** single-use hotel toiletries, or don't use them at all to leave them for the next person. Even better if you bring your own!
- **Reduce** electricity use by turning off lights and air conditioning in your accommodation when you're not there.
- **Reduce** or eliminate using private transport for short journeys that could be walked where possible (or hire a local bicycle!).
- Bring a **reusable** water bottle to refill during your trip rather than purchase multiple plastic bottles of water.
- Bring your own **reusable** shopping bag when you're out and about to minimise taking on new plastic bags.
- **Hang on** to your rubbish and correctly dispose of it according to local recommendations on recycling.
- When in Asia, bring your own **reusable** chopsticks. It's believed that 24 *billion* pairs of disposable chopsticks are used annually in Japan alone!

Ensure You Leave No Trace

Love hiking and immersing yourself in the outdoors? Chances are you may have already heard of the Leave No Trace principles. These are a set of guidelines of sustainable tourism habits to follow to ensure nature is left exactly as you found it for the benefit of local flora, fauna and future generations.

These guidelines remain the copyright of Leave No Trace Center for Outdoor Ethics so I recommend you check them out directly for further information on each of the following principles.

Seven Principles of Leave No Trace

- Plan Ahead and Prepare
- Travel and Camp on Durable Surfaces
- Dispose of Waste Properly
- Leave What You Find
- Minimize Campfire Impacts
- Respect Wildlife
- Be Considerate of Other Visitors
- © 1999 by the Leave No Trace Center for Outdoor Ethics: LNT.org[74]

Think Twice About Leaving Love Locks Behind

In my earliest travels back in 2008, it seemed love locks were an emerging trend. I visited 16 countries in Europe during that trip and have to admit I can only really remember seeing padlocks in Rome and Paris, there were very few of them. At first I didn't even know why they were there!

Fast forward to today and this trend has absolutely exploded all over the world. I understand to some it may seem like a nice idea in theory to leave a piece representing you and your lover behind forever. So why haven't I bothered leaving my mark?

I'm going to focus on Paris, France for this example, but similar situations have occured in Prague, Czech Republic and Rome, Italy.

Overloaded: Negative impacts of love locks in Paris

It's true, my individual lock probably isn't going to make much of a difference. So let's think of it this way: Paris had 24 million visitors in 2015 alone. For a moment, imagine if 24 million

PART IV: Solutions to Overtourism - During a Trip   111

people all put a lock on a bridge or structure. The extra and unaccounted-for weight will inevitably take a toll and cause irreversible harm to the structure. As we have seen in the first half of this book, individual actions collectively add up!

Some of these structures are centuries old and people are so swept away by the seemingly romantic gesture that thinking about the long-term damage their lock will do is the last thing on their minds. These beautiful structures are part of the reasons we visit a city but they will slowly decay by being inundated with rusty locks.

Let's take a look at some of reasons why it's a bad idea to leave love locks behind during your travels:

- Critics argue love locks are a form of vandalism[75] and I have to agree. Not only do they look ugly and cause damage by rusting over time due to being exposed to the elements, the keys thrown into the rivers pollute the waterways which leads to poor water quality.
- Love locks pose a hazard. According to the city of Paris, 65 tonnes of locks were removed from the Pont des Arts bridge in June 2015, and 35 tonnes from the Pont de l'Archevêché near Notre Dame cathedral.
- Each section of the guardrail on the Pont des Arts was weighed down by a whopping 330 kilograms of locks, and sections would collapse regularly. Paris City Hall decided to take action after a panel of locks on the Pont des Arts collapsed onto the walkway of the bridge, nearly injuring tourists.
- Additionally, a centuries-old lamppost on Ponte Milvio in Rome, Italy almost toppled over under the weight of these locks into the river below, prompting authorities to remove the locks as a safety precaution.
- Before the padlocks were removed from Pont des Arts in Paris, the authorities placed signs over the locks explaining why they were going to be removed. The signs read:

"The weight of your love weighs down our monuments and endangers the capital's visitors.

Because our bridges will buckle under the weight of all the love locks, the City of Paris is removing them. Since 2008, many of you have come here to pledge your love and attach locks to Parisian bridges. This actually does long-term damage to the capital's cultural heritage and creates safety problems.

As a result, the City of Paris has opted for a long-term alternative. From this autumn, the lattice grills will be replaced with glass panels which will allow the bridge to retain its transparent charm."

In cities where love locks are popular I refuse to support local businesses or street vendors who promote and sell locks for this very purpose. Why should we be supportive of people who are happy to accelerate the damage being done to icons in their very own cities? We need to help preserve these destinations, not contribute to their gradual decay and demise.

According to Lisa Anselmo of preservation group No Love Locks[76], "One man's expression of love must never come at the expense of the cultural heritage of others. When you come to another country and willingly deface a historic landmark, that is vandalism by definition. It becomes about ego, and it's morally bankrupt."

This blatant graffiti is completely disrespectful to locals, their city and is the exact opposite of being an Invisible Tourist. I'm proud to say I was one of the first travel writers to resist the love lock trend, having written a full article about why we shouldn't leave them in Paris and beyond[77] before authorities began removing them.

Are there any responsible alternatives to love locks?

Fortunately, the answer is yes! After all, leaving behind love locks is only as eternal as the time it takes for it to rust or authorities to come along with bolt cutters. Aside from destinations such as South Korea and Russia having dedicated lock sculptures created specifically for this purpose, we'll delve deeper into other alternatives in the next section about local souvenirs.

Purchase Local Handicrafts as Souvenirs

A better alternative to leaving love locks behind at your destination is to take a piece of the destination home with you. I'm not in any way saying to steal ancient rocks from the Acropolis or fill a jar with sand from a beach in Barcelona. No, no, no.

By this I mean purchase a unique, authentic souvenir from a small local business. Anything that hasn't been mass-produced and has been created with thought and care will help you remember your visit meaningfully. Not only does this help support local jobs and artisans, it can keep old traditions alive which makes up part of the reasons why each destination is unique.

Treat yourself some of these items by talented local creators:

- Textiles and fabrics
- Artisan foods such as cakes, crackers, sweets
- Handmade jewellery
- Homewares such as ceramics, small glass items
- Paintings and other artworks
- Handmade lucky charms
- Christmas decorations
- Even partaking in a local cooking class is a souvenir that will last a lifetime!

As well as your photos and memories, I believe these are the types of things we should be bringing home with us. We are free to use these things whenever we like and remind us of our fond time on our trip, rather than wondering if our rusty padlock we left on some European bridge fell victim to bolt cutters from authorities, without the chance of ever seeing or finding it again.

Souvenirs not to buy

Not all souvenirs are good for the local community or environment. Simply put, we can use our hidden power to influence change here. If tourists don't buy them, vendors won't want to sell them. Where possible, try to avoid mass produced trinkets made outside of the destination because these don't go far towards giving back to the communities who live and work there.

Being an Invisible Tourist is also about doing what we can to protect the local environment, this includes avoiding souvenirs made from endangered animal species. Purchasing these kinds of items can result in confiscation or a hefty fine at your departure point if importing or exporting the item is illegal. Souvenirs not to buy include, but aren't limited to:

- **Exotic animal skins, furs:** The inhumane nature of obtaining the skins means they are no longer widely accepted fashion
- **Ivory:** 33,000 elephants are killed for their tusks every year according to WildAid[78]
- **Tortoiseshell items:** Created from the endangered Hawksbill turtle
- **Seashells, coral:** These can be illegally harvested and cause damage to local ecosystems
- **Rosewood items:** An endangered hardwood obtained by illegal logging and used in furniture
- **Shatoosh:** A traditional shawl from Himalayas, woven from endangered Tibetan antelope 'chiru' wool.

Participate in Cultural Experiences

After making my way through the maze of hallways that is Apostolic Palace in Vatican City, I gasped as I finally passed beneath the large doorway into the Sistine Chapel. Trying to block out security guards warning *"Silenzio! Put the camer-a in the bag-a"* piercing through the low hum of visitors' movements every few moments, I eventually found a seat off to the side where I could just stop and gaze at what was before my eyes.

This was it, I was finally here. One of the very first places I was inspired to visit from the *Handbook of Art* as a young girl. There was so much more detail to admire than I had imagined! Through an aching neck fixed upwards, my eyes searched for some time until I finally found *that* famous image of *The Creation of Adam*, his bare body outreaching a fingertip to touch God floating beside him, surrounded by cherubs.

Within the chapel, being able to grasp the sheer scale of work by Michelangelo's own hand literally took my breath away. To think all this painstaking work eventually rendered him blind! The 500-year old painted frescoes on this ceiling and adorning the chapel's walls will forever be one of the most incredible things I have ever seen.

For a few moments my mind was whisked away to Italy during the Renaissance period, and I understood why Michelangelo was such a beloved figure throughout Italy even to this day.

Now, remember earlier in Part IV I explained why cultural experiences are one of my favourite things about being a tourist? Now's your chance to enjoy the activities you booked in advance! Immersing yourself in the local culture is the perfect way to gain a greater understanding about the destination, its history and its people. Isn't that what travel is supposed to be all about?

Museums and art galleries

While art galleries and museums are an acquired taste for some, I really can't recommend visiting them enough to help you appreciate the significance of the featured pieces to the local population's cultural heritage. The key is to allow enough time to read about the artefacts so you don't end up rushing through and missing valuable information.

There is nothing more inspiring than walking out bursting with knowledge about how different cultures lived in the past, intriguing stories behind artworks and events that shaped our lives to this day.

With the exception of the State Hermitage Museum in Russia's St Petersburg, I was inspired by the *Handbook of Art* textbook to visit the world-class museums and galleries listed below. If you ever have the chance, take the plunge and visit for yourself - there is a reason why they are famous, after all!

- Foundation de Claude Monet - Giverny, France
- Musée du Louvre - Paris, France
- Musée d'Orsay - Paris, France
- Château de Versailles - Versailles, France
- Deutsches Historisches Museum - Berlin, Germany
- Acropolis Museum - Athens, Greece
- Ohara Museum of Art - Kurashiki, Japan
- Anne Frank Huis - Amsterdam, Netherlands
- Rijksmuseum - Amsterdam, Netherlands
- Van Gogh Museum - Amsterdam, Netherlands
- Casa Milà - Barcelona, Spain
- Museo del Prado - Madrid, Spain
- British Museum - London, United Kingdom
- National Gallery - London, United Kingdom
- Metropolitan Museum of Art - New York City, United States
- Museum of Modern Art (MoMA) - New York City, United States

- Smithsonian Institution - Washington DC, United States
- State Hermitage Museum - St Petersburg, Russia
- Sistine Chapel - Vatican City.

The best part is money from your visit helps to contribute to the upkeep of the museum, gallery or local business while employing locals passionate about their workplace.

TIP: Museum gift shops also tend to have quite unique souvenirs as well!

Cooking classes and other traditional activities

In a quiet backstreet of a Kyoto neighbourhood, I began salivating in anticipation of creating my very own bowl of ramen noodles from scratch. I'm definitely not the best in the kitchen (hey, I'm good at other things!) so it was good to know my upcoming Japanese cooking class would walk me through the process step-by-step.

A wave of relief washed over me when I saw the clear instruction booklet on my table, numerous ingredients measured out before me and ready to go. Prior to this day, I'd never really thought about just how many ingredients went into cooking a single bowl of ramen!

This next part made me REALLY appreciate people who created noodles from scratch in previous centuries, and who still do so today. After following the instructions my noodle dough was ready. "Now, you must punch it one hundred times before rolling flat," my hostess instructed with a giggle. That's right, dear reader, ONE HUNDRED times. With force.

I thought I'd already had my fair share of a workout carting my suitcase up staircases in *ryokans* (B&Bs) during that Japan trip. The punching part really burned my upper arms, no word of a lie! To make it a little easier on myself, I punched the dough

10-15 times before folding it over and repeating the process. And you know what? It was the best ramen I had ever tasted. If you're a foodie, you're bound to love being hands-on at your destination by joining a local cooking class. As mentioned earlier, learning to cook a local specialty yourself makes a wonderful souvenir.

Learning more about culture through food helps you better understand the connection locals have with their environment, as well as supporting small businesses and sampling the local produce in the process.

TIP: Rather not cook yourself? Joining a local foodie walking tour is another great way to sample the local cuisine of a destination whilst learning more about it. Having a local show you the ropes from the beginning will give you the confidence to get out more on your own later in the trip, too.

More examples of culturally immersive experiences

From centuries old traditions still practiced today to more modern activities, these are just a few examples of cultural experiences you could get involved in during your future trip:

- Enjoy a handmade chocolate workshop in Belgium
- Learn about the national alcoholic beverage of choice on a sake brewery tour in Japan
- Get involved in 13th century tradition that is the Venice Carnival in Italy
- Explore the opulent Château de Versailles to see how royalty once lived in France
- Savour dinner and a traditional Maori cultural performance at Rotorua in New Zealand
- Attend the annual *Almabtrieb* alpine decorated cattle procession in Austria.

Intangible cultural heritage

Did you know there is a term used to describe immaterial and non-physical things relating to culture? Known as *intangible cultural heritage*, this can be defined as a practice, representation, expression, knowledge, tradition, folklore, belief, skill or even language that is fundamental to a destination's culture and identity.

You never know what experience you may stumble across during your trip. It's a great idea to check the local tourism board's website for any events that may coincide with your visit. When you do, be sure to properly check the dates - words of wisdom I learnt the hard way.

I'd planned an entire trip to Brussels, Belgium to see their incredible *Tapis de Fleur* (Flower Carpet) in its old town square known as the Grand Place. After I'd booked everything for the trip I realised the festival is only held every *second* year - and not the year I was going to be there. Oops.

Anyway, do a little research and get involved to experience something truly unforgettable!

Examples of UNESCO Intangible Cultural Heritage around the globe include:
- Yama, Hoko and Yatai float festivals in Japan
- Craftsmanship of mechanical watchmaking in Switzerland and France
- Handmade production of Christmas tree decorations from blown glass beads in Czech Republic
- Sauna culture in Finland
- Byzantine chants of Cyprus and Greece
- Irish harping in Ireland
- Traditional skills of crafting and playing Dotar in Iran
- Traditional archery in Turkey
- Argungu fishing and cultural festival in Nigeria.

If Posting to Social Media, Remember to Do So in an Ethical Way

This is an important thing I feel isn't talked about as much as it should be. Some time ago I remember reading an Instagram post from a fellow travel blogger saying she'd spent all day wandering around her destination trying to acquire a suitable photo to share. It saddened me to think this was the purpose of her day - there is SO much more to travelling than posting photos to social media!

Call me old-fashioned, but as someone who travelled well before smartphones and Facebook I tend not to even think about posting to social media until after I've returned home. Sure, I love to capture amazing shots as much as the next person, however that should never be the *sole purpose* of travel. Sometimes the best travel memories are the ones we keep to ourselves.

Hastily-added photos online have caused a number of issues you may never have thought of. Here are some ways you can be a more mindful and ethical tourist when it comes to posting on social media.

Stop geotagging

Yes, I'm being serious. As mentioned previously Instagram has been one of the driving forces behind the rise of tourism in recent years, with 57% of people in a survey[79] admitting they were interested in travelling somewhere that would "look good" in social media pictures.

Geotagged locations made it all too easy for folks to flock to a location en masse without knowing the significance of the place aside from it being a pretty photo opportunity. There's no reward without work. Help protect the location by making people go to the effort of researching it for themselves and they may learn a few important things.

Always ask for permission to photograph local people

When it comes to photography, always ask locals if they are comfortable having their photo taken before you snap away. While it may seem harmless to capture candid photos of local people, I know I personally don't want an unauthorised photo of myself splashed across a random person's social media page. Do you?

I can't help but think back to the "Afghan Girl" story[80] who appeared on the cover of National Geographic magazine. It's important to respect privacy so it's ethical to blur out faces in photos of locals you didn't receive permission from (you may notice this in photos of crowds on my blog).

In Japan, it is against the law to photograph people without their consent. It stems back to an incident where a wife caught her husband with a mistress from a photo of him shared on social media. He took the case to court and won. Crop out identifying features and don't land yourself in trouble!

Avoid risky encounters with wild animals

Animal "selfies" are popular on social media. However, the extremes some people have gone to in order to achieve these shots have resulted in hospital visits.

In Nara, Japan, over 200 injuries were recorded in 2018 from tourists teasing the sacred deer with food to lure them closer for selfies. Similarly in Yellowstone National Park in the United States, bison have charged at groups[81] of people who have been too close, even flipping a 9 year old girl and goring a 62 year old man.

Wild animals are just that: wild and unpredictable. Please remember to admire these creatures from afar instead of risking injuries and encouraging others to achieve such photos.

Avoid placing yourself in avoidable situations

Cliff edges, boiling geysers, oncoming traffic and scaling structures illegally may gain you some social media attention, however placing yourself in these situations can sometimes cost you a prison sentence or even your life. If you have a young and impressionable audience, your actions may be justification for others to do the same.

Know your limits. Be aware of your surroundings, any hazards and abide by local signage to not be an irresponsible tourist.

Overview: During a Trip

Thanks to our solid preparation before we stepped foot on foreign soil, we know exactly what we need to do to better *blend in* amongst locals during our trip. We're certain to have the most enjoyable experience possible by ensuring we are:

- Dressing appropriately for the destination we are visiting.
- Practising local customs and etiquette to demonstrate our cultural awareness.
- Familiarising ourselves with a few language basics to show we respect locals, and for ease of communication in essential day-to-day interactions.
- Exploring with a healthy dose of skepticism, alertness, and refraining from displaying large amounts of cash to avoid pickpockets and scammers.
- Using public transport (outside of busy hours) instead of private transfers to get around, save money and experience the local way of life.
- Not carrying a selfie stick or a huge camera around that makes it obvious we are tourists.
- Being mindful about dining at (and purchasing from) small businesses to support locals, their families, and to reduce economic leakage.
- Embracing the Leave No Trace principles and minimising

our environmental impacts by reducing, reusing and recycling where possible.
- Finding local handicrafts to purchase as souvenirs rather than leaving behind love locks that permanently damage historical structures.
- Ethically posting to social media (if at all) without geotagging, always asking permission to photograph local people, avoiding risky encounters with wild animals and not placing ourselves in avoidable situations.

AFTER A TRIP

How to Enjoy the Tourist Experience from Home

Armed with the knowledge you've gained throughout this handbook, let's take a moment to fast-forward to the future. Having now hypothetically implemented all the advice in the real world, imagine you've just returned from your first trip as a *true* Invisible Tourist. What a journey it was!

But is there a way you can keep that buzzing feeling and love for travel ongoing once you're back home?

It can be sad once the after-holiday glow becomes a distant memory as we settle back into reality. Which is probably why planning your next trip not long after you return is so addictive - I know this first-hand!

While nothing can completely replace being at a destination in person, I'm pleased to suggest there are ways you can still enjoy the tourist experience from home to keep the exciting spirit of travel alive when you're not on the road.

Here are a few suggestions that have helped me feel connected to my favourite destinations when I can't be there in person. Hopefully these ideas can tide you over until your next trip!

Enjoy Tangible Souvenirs at Home

Dedicate an area of your home to souvenirs you've collected during your travels. Perhaps it may be a bookshelf or side table to display your trinkets, or you prefer to have them spread out in different locations around your home. This is especially true for wall-hanging souvenirs such as paintings, posters or fabrics.

Remember back to how you felt when you first saw it; the events of that day; the new things you experienced. It's so lovely to be surrounded by things that evoke nostalgia from your adventures!

Take Online Cooking classes or Use a Recipe Learnt During Your Travels

Have you heard it's possible to take online cooking classes with locals at different destinations around the globe? All you need are your ingredients and a connection to a webcam enabled device!

I've written in detail about my online Japanese cooking class[82] where I made gyoza (dumplings) with a lovely local lady from Tokyo in real time. There are benefits to taking live online classes rather than watching a YouTube video about the same thing, such as the ability to ask your host questions along the way and enjoy exchanging stories about your travels.

If you did take a cooking class at the destination on a previous trip, have a country-specific themed night at home and try out the recipe you learnt. The aromas and flavours will take you back to your experience at the destination, a fun way to relive the excitement!

Undertake Virtual Travel Experiences

I know virtual tours aren't the same as *actually* being at the destination, however they're a great way to forge connections with locals and learn insider tips you may not have found on your own. Having a local show you around the destination online in real time is probably the best way to experience the place without physically being there.

Live virtual tours will give you ideas for places to go and things to see when you get the chance to visit in future, plus the opportunity to ask questions about any mistakes to avoid. From local guided tours in a city to the world's major museums and galleries holding their own tours online, grab yourself some snacks, take notes and allow your mind to be whisked away.

Pick Up a Language Class

As we examined earlier, there are free and paid resources to help expand your vocabulary to include words and phrases from your target destination.

Your teacher will likely have spent an extended amount of time at the destination and will have plenty of tips and advice to share about upping your language game. Knowing you'll be able to practice these words in person someday is an exciting thing to look forward to. Build your confidence by getting linguistically prepared for when you revisit!

Read the Destination's Local News Online

Reading the local news online is a great way to maintain a connection to the destination by staying up-to-date with current affairs and events. It's also perfect for staying informed about new places that have opened to add to your list for visiting in future (or places that have closed), political situations, and more.

TIP: Don't forget to read any comments left by locals on articles or accompanying social media to better understand their thoughts on a news story or situation.

Read Books About the Destination

Whether fiction or non-fiction, reading books about the destination is a great mental escape. You'll be able to picture areas more vividly having visited yourself, and it may mention new places you can daydream about exploring during your next visit. The same can be said for watching TV shows and movies, too - get excited about areas you saw in person!

Sign Up to a Travel-Themed Subscription Box

Craving a particular snack from your previous travels, but can't get back there anytime soon? In recent years the number of destination-themed subscription boxes has been steadily rising. They're wonderful for bringing snacks to you that are difficult to find outside of the destination.

Simply sign up with your preferred supplier and pay a monthly fee to have a box of themed goodies delivered directly to your door. Boxes include destination-specific snacks, treats, sweets, trinkets, and even small homewares.

Websites such as CrateJoy feature a huge range of different boxes from around the globe. If you're specifically interested in Japan, my reviews for trendy snacks with TokyoTreat[83] and traditional sweets with Sakuraco[84] detail what to expect from these subscription services.

The added benefit (aside from the amazing goodies) is supporting local businesses at the destination. I especially loved creating a Japan-themed picnic at home with Sakuraco's traditional treats box knowing I was supporting the traditional artisans in Japan who created them!

Create Photobooks or Scrapbooks of Your Trips

Photobooks are a sure-fire way to ignite a decent dose of nostalgia from your trip. Let's face it, most of us forget the small details of our trips so browsing through the pictures and re-reading little notes we wrote helps to fondly remember and relive those experiences. Sites such as Blurb are great for this.

Other Ideas

If you enjoy looking back on your travels from time to time, consider investing in a travel journal to take with you on future adventures. I received one as a gift many years ago and it journeyed with me around the world until I filled all its pages! My journal also has a little pocket in its inside back cover to store old tickets I collected during my time away.

My nightly ritual during each trip I took included taking a few moments to jot down what I got up to throughout the day. Did I try any local specialties with interesting names? Fascinating things about someone I met? Recommendations from locals to remember when revisiting someday? Important cultural differences or facts to take note of? Funny encounters or things I heard that only seem to happen when abroad?

Even to this day I pull out the travel journal every so often and laugh at amusing things I wrote all those years ago. It's heartwarming and nostalgic to think back to those small details I had forgotten over time, but had immortalised through my writings. I highly recommend you grab one, your future self will thank you for it years down the track!

Your Responsibility as a Tourist After a Trip

I'm not sure about you, but I absolutely *love* chatting about my travel experiences with friends and family once I return home. So much so, I'm pretty sure they all tired of hearing it so I created my blog to share it all with a larger audience, ha!

I want to share the benefits of the experiences, the emotions I felt, and interesting pieces of information I learnt along the way so others can one day feel this same fulfilment during their own travels.

With that said, I believe we have a responsibility to inform other potential tourists about things we see during our travels that don't seem right. It's important to share the good as well as the bad so things can improve.

Sometimes the easiest way to solve a problem is to stop participating in it. Remember to tap into your hidden power and voice your concerns to help drive positive change in an industry where we, as tourists, lead the way.

CONCLUSION

Recalling how the famous fairytale of the *Little Mermaid* was written by Danish author Hans Christian Andersen, it was humbling to think I now stood before a tangible connection to it. I pictured Carl Jacobsen attending the Royal Danish Theatre ballet performance of Andersen's story - a mermaid who gave up everything to be united with a young, handsome prince. It was Jacobsen falling in love with the ballet's main character that ultimately inspired him to commission the statue.

Now over 100 years later, I was here to see this unique landmark, feeling a connection to the history, the story, the importance of it all to the culture of Denmark. The precious gift that is the privilege of being able to explore this beautiful world we call home.

I've been fortunate enough to benefit from the global tourism boom, especially since the turn of the 21st century where the Internet, technology, increased competition and even social media has revolutionised the way in which we all travel.

While these factors made it easier than ever to explore our globe, they also detached tourists from what it meant to have meaningful experiences. Somehow along the way, we started to value a selfie more than a sunset; we preferred to take photos of our food instead of savouring the flavours; we cared more about getting "likes" instead of living in the moment.

Furthermore, increased pressure on local resources, infrastructure and the depleting supply of long-term rental properties has damaged locals' quality of life and led to destinations becoming victims of their own success. Not only can the actions of too many tourists drive locals out of their own cities, it can often lead to unfulfillment and disappointment for everyone involved.

In the same way that we are highly aware of negative ecological effects on our natural environment, we must recognise impacts that overtourism can have on the cultural identity of a local community. After all, it is often the unique importance of a destination's cultural heritage that drew tourists in the first place.

Laying my head to rest on my pillow during my final night in Copenhagen, I thought back to the *Little Mermaid*'s story. Swimming to the surface every morning and evening from the sea's depths, she stares longingly from her rock towards the shore hoping to catch a glimpse of her beloved prince. In the same way us tourists keep coming back; keep journeying to escape our mundane routine existence; spreading out across the world, hoping to fulfil a beautiful experience that drives us.

Then I am reminded of relentless commotion as the flock of tourists scramble over water and boulders for their photo op, and I decide then and there that we can - and need - to do better than this. It all starts by awakening the hidden power within us.

***

ACKNOWLEDGEMENTS

To my ARC Team, for throwing your support behind this book the moment I mentioned its existence; for reading my drafts and providing detailed feedback to help make it the best it could be (with a special mention to Van and Rob). The entire process would not have been possible without your time, input and dedication, for this I owe each and every one of you my deepest thanks.

To my partner and ultimate travel buddy, for sharing almost every adventure with me described in this book. There aren't enough words to express how thankful I am that you allow me to drag you around the world at times. How appreciative I am for you listening to me talk tirelessly about my blog and writing this book. How indebted I am to you for being my mentor and providing me with advice I need to hear to achieve my goals. Your opinions (even the unpopular ones) are always respected and keep me grounded. I'm so grateful you're my one in seven billion.

To each of my grandfathers - Grandpa, by becoming a pilot you no doubt subconsciously inspired my endless love of travel; and Pa, for taking a leap of faith to journey a world away from Italy to begin a new life in Australia after the second world war. The choices and sacrifices made by you both helped shape the person I am today, and remind me anything is possible with hard work and determination.

To my parents, thank you for always backing my crazy ambitions and cheering on my successes. To my family and closest friends, you've shown your support for The Invisible Tourist since day one, it means the world. To Stella, for your unrivalled honesty when it comes to bouncing off ideas for behind-the-scenes work to do with The Invisible Tourist. You've always got my back.

To Nayer, thank you for first igniting the spark within me to bring this book into existence. I hope you find it a useful resource for how to be an Invisible Tourist and refer to it often.

To Sylvia of Spin the Globe, thank you for your time contributing to the mini interview in this book around Accessible Travel, your insights on this topic are greatly appreciated.

To all readers of The Invisible Tourist, past and present, for your increasing interest in travelling responsibly to help preserve local cultures that make us all unique. It's you I credit for transforming my passion into a career I never dreamed possible only a few years ago. For this I will be forever grateful.

To Whittaker's Chocolates and Japanese sake brewers for creating the fuel I needed to burn during tireless nights figuring out how to write and publish a book.

Finally, I send a bittersweet thanks to all the annoying tourists I've encountered during my trips. Without them I would not have been inspired to write this book!

LIKE THIS BOOK?
LEAVE A REVIEW!

If you found the information provided in this handbook helpful, I'd love if you could spare a moment to leave a review as a show of thanks and to spread the word :)

https://www.amazon.com/dp/B09D2WKXDL/

Whether it's to come and say hello, start a discussion or follow along, come and join me over on my social media platforms to stay up-to-date with my latest work:
Facebook: https://www.facebook.com/theinvisibletourist/
Instagram: https://www.instagram.com/theinvisibletourist/
Pinterest: https://www.pinterest.com.au/theinvisibletourist/
TikTok: https://www.tiktok.com/@theinvisibletourist

Don't forget to use the *#invisibletourism* hashtag on your favourite social media platform when posting about your travels using my advice in this book - I always love to hear from you.

Head over to my blog https://www.theinvisibletourist.com for more travel inspiration or simply scan the image below. I hope to see you again soon!

ABOUT THE AUTHOR

Australian-based Alyse is founder of The Invisible Tourist, the No.1 travel blog that has encouraged tourists to better *blend in* on their travels. Documenting her journeys around the globe by being *invisible*, Alyse's advice is especially popular with visitors to Japan and has helped millions of tourists enrich their travel experiences since her blog's founding in 2017.

Alyse was a "Japan Guru" guest speaker at the Klook Travel & Japan Rail Pass Workshop event in Sydney, Australia in 2020. Her work has been featured by AmericanExpress Essentials, Tokyo Broadcasting System (TBS Japan), Klook Travel, Refinery29, European Union Eco-Tandem Programme, Scott's Cheap Flights and more.

Follow her adventures at theinvisibletourist.com or join the *#invisibletourism* movement on social media.

BIBLIOGRAPHY & FURTHER READING

PART II

1. https://data.worldbank.org/indicator/ST.INT.ARVL
2. https://www.weforum.org/agenda/2020/07/the-rise-of-the-asian-middle-class/
3. https://www.statista.com/chart/8402/asian-middle-class-on-the-rise/
4. https://www.bbc.com/news/business-22037233
5. https://www.businessinsider.com/how-low-cost-airlines-are-changing-the-face-of-air-travel-2018-7?r=AU&IR=T
6. https://www.bbc.com/news/magazine-34722176
7. https://thepointsguy.com/news/why-cruise-ships-keep-getting-bigger/
8. https://www.npr.org/2019/06/02/729075426/massive-cruise-ship-crashes-into-port-in-venice-injuring-at-least-5
9. https://www.usatoday.com/story/tech/2016/03/14/anti-airbnb-lobby-doubles-spending/81762374/
10. https://www.airbnbhell.com/tag/airbnb-illegal-listing/
11. https://www.heraldtribune.com/news/20180827/airbnb-and-partner-buying-apartment-complexes
12. https://www.bloomberg.com/news/articles/2018-03-05/what-airbnb-did-to-new-york-city-s-housing-market
13. https://www.businessofapps.com/data/airbnb-statistics/
14. https://spintheglobe.net/
15. https://www.kiwi.com/stories/study-suggests-people-travel-for-likes/
16. https://www.theinvisibletourist.com/dos-and-donts-in-bali-travel-tips-indonesia/
17. https://matadornetwork.com/read/two-thirds-americans-vacation-lies/
18. https://www.forbes.com/sites/andrewarnold/2018/01/24/heres-how-much-instagram-likes-influence-millennials-choice-of-travel-destinations/#36c7a6e04eba
19. https://www.theguardian.com/environment/2019/mar/18/super-bloom-lake-elsinore-poppies-flowers
20. https://www.bbc.com/news/newsbeat-45745982

21. https://www.secretflying.com/posts/french-economy-class-influencer-mocked-for-faking-business-class-trip/
22. https://travel.nine.com.au/latest/influencers-private-jet-set-fake-photos/ac0b77f4-c9cc-45ac-880b-55a8b9c81571
23. https://mipon.org/what-is-anime-pilgrimage-and-anime-tourism/

PART III

24. https://www.responsibletravel.com/holidays/the-netherlands/travel-guide/overtourism-in-amsterdam
25. https://responsibletravel.com/copy/overtourism-in-barcelona
26. https://www.thelocal.it/20161015/cardinals-up-in-arms-over-st-peters-square-mcdonalds
27. https://www.responsibletravel.com/holidays/the-netherlands/travel-guide/overtourism-in-amsterdam
28. https://newleftreview.org/issues/ii88/articles/marco-d-eramo-unescocide
29. https://www.theguardian.com/cities/2017/aug/30/unescocide-world-heritage-status-hurt-help-tourism
30. https://www.gdrc.org/uem/eco-tour/envi/one.html
31. https://www.express.co.uk/news/world/850331/Croatia-tourism-clampdown-protect-Dubrovnic
32. https://www.responsibletravel.com/copy/overtourism-in-venice
33. https://knoema.com/atlas/topics/Tourism/Travel-and-Tourism-Total-Contribution-to-GDP/Contribution-of-travel-and-tourism-to-GDP-percent-of-GDP
34. https://en.unesco.org/courier/2017-april-june/angkor-water-crisis
35. https://soranews24.com/2020/01/13/japanese-shrine-bans-foreign-visitors-following-disrespectful-behaviour-by-tourists/
36. https://www.bloomberg.com/news/articles/2019-02-19/why-lisbon-can-t-stop-its-azulejo-thieves
37. https://www.worldanimalprotection.org/news/exposed-true-scale-thailands-tiger-selfie-tourism
38. https://www.peta.org/issues/animals-in-entertainment/circuses/
39. https://www.abc.net.au/news/2018-04-20/kangaroo-dies-in-chinese-zoo-after-visitors-throw-rocks/9682220

40. https://theboar.org/2019/11/the-dark-side-of-animal-tourism
41. https://www.dailymail.co.uk/news/article-2321181/British-tourists-charged-54-ice-creams-receive-apology-invited-Rome-mayor.html
42. https://www.thelocal.es/20190606/barcelona-and-palma-ranked-worst-in-europe-for-cruise-ship-pollution.
43. https://foe.org/news/2014-12-cruise-ships-flushed-more-than-a-billion-gallons-of-sewage-into-oceans/
44. https://www.nature.com/articles/s41598-019-55238-z
45. https://www.nytimes.com/2019/06/03/travel/traveling-climate-change.html
46. https://savethechildren.org.au/our-stories/the-truth-about-voluntourism
47. http://pepytours.com/volunteering-in-cambodia-interview-with-daniela-papi/
48. https://www.theguardian.com/news/2018/sep/13/the-business-of-voluntourism-do-western-do-gooders-actually-do-harm
49. https://www.aph.gov.au/Parliamentary_Business/Committees/Joint/Foreign_Affairs_Defence_and_Trade/ModernSlavery/Final_report/section?id=committees%2Freportjnt%2F024102%2F25036
50. https://www.insider.com/bali-tourist-spot-popular-instagram-fake-photo-op-2019-7
51. https://www.theguardian.com/environment/2019/oct/27/super-rich-fuelling-growing-demand-for-private-jets-report-finds
52. https://www.ecotravelist.com/blog/how-to-spot-greenwashing-in-the-travel-industry

PART IV

53. https://theinvisibletourist.com/best-month-to-visit-paris-revealed/
54. https://theinvisibletourist.com/planning-a-trip-to-japan-travel-tips/
55. https://theinvisibletourist.com/7-days-in-switzerland-itinerary/
56. https://theinvisibletourist.com/invisible-tourist-vs-traveller/
57. https://www.independent.ie/business/personal-finance/property-mortgages/rise-of-64pc-in-rental-properties-across-dublin-in-midst-of-coronavirus-crisis-daft-report-39061809.html
58. https://www.theguardian.com/world/2018/jun/15/tourism-pollution-backlash-japan-crackdown-costs-airbnb-10m-kyoto
59. http://news.com.au/finance/real-estate/renting/

illegal-airbnb-subletting-exposed/news-story/7313a9518e70ac066b3a395340d11a60

60. http://insideairbnb.com/paris/
61. https://mashable.com/2017/12/04/airbnb-host-spying-webcam/#Mb_YHO2y8mqM
62. https://www.airbnbhell.com/?s=bait+and+switch
63. https://www.reddit.com/r/travel/comments/2em0ay/why_wont_you_use_airbnb/
64. https://mainichi.jp/english/articles/20200618/p2a/00m/0na/025000c
65. https://theinvisibletourist.com/is-klook-legit-book-travel-experiences/
66. https://www.worldanimalprotection.org.au/wildlife-not-entertainers/worlds-cruellest-attractions?from=international_en
67. https://www.peta.org/features/real-animal-sanctuary-zoo/
68. https://brainybackpackers.com/unethical-animal-tourism/
69. https://www.tripadvisor.com.au/ShowUserReviews-g274707-d607219-r184449350-Karlovy_Lazne-Prague_Bohemia.html
70. https://theinvisibletourist.com/responsible-tourism-be-invisible/
71. https://www.justtheflight.co.uk/blog/16-40-tourist-scams-to-avoid-this-summer.html
72. https://theguardian.com/world/2018/dec/21/paris-charles-de-gaulle-airport-bring-in-new-taxi-scheme-after-thai-couple-charged-220-fare
73. http://www.scmp.com/news/china/article/1249285/robberies-cashed-chinese-tourists-rise-steeply-paris
74. http://www.lnt.org
75. http://www.telegraph.co.uk/travel/destinations/europe/france/paris/articles/Paris-Love-locks-are-vandalism-and-should-be-banned/
76. https://nolovelocks.com/en/
77. https://theinvisibletourist.com/why-ill-never-leave-love-locks-in-paris/
78. https://wildaid.org/programs/elephants/
79. https://www.livemint.com/technology/tech-news/gen-z-takes-to-instagram-for-deciding-on-holiday-destination-1563952379083.html
80. https://thewire.in/media/afghan-girl-steve-mccurry-national-geographic
81. https://www.iflscience.com/plants-and-animals/bison-seriously-injures-second-tourist-three-weeks-yellowstone-national-park/
82. https://theinvisibletourist.com/japanese-cooking-class-online/

83. https://theinvisibletourist.com/tokyo-treat-discount-code-review/
84. https://theinvisibletourist.com/japanese-sweets-sakuraco-review/

FURTHER READING

Websites
1. https://tourismteacher.com/environmental-impacts-of-tourism/
2. https://www.conserve-energy-future.com/how-tourism-affects-environment.php
3. https://daily.jstor.org/the-high-environmental-costs-of-cruise-ships/
4. https://www.travindy.com/2016/05/tourism-and-biodiversity-loss-the-threat-of-invasive-species/

Reports
1. The Ocean Conservancy - *How Cruise Ships Affect the Marine Environment* (2002): http://www.cruiseresearch.org/Cruise%20Control.pdf
2. CIHEAM International Centre for Advanced Mediterranean Agronomic Studies - *Environmental Impacts of Tourism* (2003): https://om.ciheam.org/om/pdf/a57/04001977.pdf
3. American Journal of Environment, Energy and Power Research - *Environmental Effects of Tourism* (2013): http://www.ajeepr.com/AJEEPR_Vol.%201,%20No.%208,%20September%202013/ENVIRONMENTAL.pdf
4. International Journal of Tourism Research - *The Negative Impacts of Volunteer Tourism* (2009): https://www.researchgate.net/publication/227907035_The_Possible_Negative_Impacts_of_Volunteer_Tourism

Books
1. David Huddart & Tim Stott - *Adventure Tourism: Environmental Impacts & Management* (2020)
2. David Huddart & Tim Stott - *Outdoor Recreation: Environmental Impacts & Management* (2019)
3. John Urry & Jonas Larson - *The Tourist Gaze 3.0* (2012)
4. Michael Welham - *The Tourist Trap: Wild Animals in Tourism & Voluntourism* (2020).

CPSIA information can be obtained
at www.ICGtesting.com
Printed in the USA
BVHW071140021221
623082BV00012B/190